volume 7   16 Enrichment Presentations

the complete guide to
Godly Play

Jerome W. Berryman

An imaginative method for presenting scripture stories to children

The scripture quotations used in this work are from the *Revised Standard Version of the Bible.* Old Testament Section
© 1952; New Testament Section, First Edition, © 1946; Second Edition, © 1971 by the Division of Christian Education of the
National Council of Churches of Christ in the USA.

ISBN: 978-1-9319-6046-5

TABLE OF CONTENTS

INTRODUCTION

Welcome to *Volume 7* of *The Complete Guide to Godly Play*. In this volume we gather 16 enrichment lessons to help tell the story of the church after Pentecost by focusing on the communion of saints. *Volume 1* of the series, *How to Lead Godly Play Lessons*, provides an in-depth overview of the process and method of Godly Play. Below, you'll find only quick reminder notes. Please refer to *Volume 1* for an in-depth presentation.

Following this Introduction, you'll find all the information you need to present these enrichment lessons to the children in your Godly Play room. We hope the simple format will enable all teachers, whether new or experienced, to find the information they need to enter fully into the most rewarding play we share: Godly Play.

In the presentation of the "Circle of the Church Year" (*Volume 2*) "the three great times" are identified: the mystery of Christmas, the mystery of Easter, and the mystery of Pentecost. This volume is devoted to the communion of saints as part of the Pentecost mystery.

In the same way that there is a shelf unit for the mystery of Christmas, and the mystery of Easter there also needs to be one for the mystery of Pentecost in a well-developed Godly Play classroom. To provide an overview for this volume, we will first describe what this shelf unit involves.

THE PENTECOST SHELF

The Pentecost shelf unit should ideally be close to the end of the New Testament Sacred Story shelves, because it carries the story on from there. On the top shelf looking from left to right we find the lesson about getting ready to come close to the mystery of Pentecost which contains the resurrection appearances of Jesus (*Volume 8*). This presents not only the continuation of Easter, but is also a preparation to come close to the mystery of Pentecost. Next to that, reading from left to right, we find the Pentecost lesson in the red box (*Volume 4*), and finally the Introduction to the Communion of Saints (*Volume 7*). This lesson is on a tray and contains a basket with a figure for each of the saints, a map of the world, a time line and flags of the countries the children would visit if they wanted learn more about a particular saint. On the lower shelves of the Pentecost shelf unit you place all of the lessons about the saints.

A NOTE ABOUT THE HISTORICITY OF SAINTS

Some saints have only dim historical records. "St." Valentine is an example. The record is so confusing and sparse that in 1969 St. Valentine's Day was dropped from the Roman calendar of feasts to be celebrated worldwide. Most of the saints remembered in *The Complete Guide to Godly Play, Volume 7*, have clear historical records, but even if there is a lot of pious legend involved there are good reasons to remember such people. In the case of Valentine it lends depth and meaning to Valentine's Day which is widely celebrated today for commercial and other mundane reasons.

WHEN TO TELL THESE STORIES

These lessons are for children in middle to late childhood (please see pages 18-19 in this volume). They deal with issues these children are more conscious of, and the material assumes the ability to read.

The lessons can be told:
- on All Saints' Day if your tradition celebrates this moment in the church year
- on the day your church remembers a particular saint or hero
- anytime after Easter
- when a child raises a question that the story of one of the saints might help the child to explore

WHAT IS GODLY PLAY?

Godly Play is what Jerome Berryman calls his interpretation of Montessori religious education. It is an imaginative approach to working with children that supports, challenges, nourishes and guides their spiritual quest. It is more akin to a spiritual practice than to what we generally think of as religious education.

Godly Play assumes that children have some experience of the mystery of the presence of God in their lives, but understands that often in our culture they lack the language, permission and understanding to express and enjoy it. In Godly Play, we enter into parables, silence, sacred stories and liturgical action to discover God, ourselves, one another and the sacredness around us.

In Godly Play, we prepare a special environment for children to work in with adult guides. Two teachers guide the session, making time for the children:
- to enter the space and be greeted
- to get ready for the presentation
- to enter into a presentation based on a parable, sacred story or liturgical action
- to respond to the presentation through shared wondering
- to respond to the presentation (or other significant spiritual issues) with their own work, either expressive art or with the lesson materials
- to prepare and share a feast
- to say goodbye and leave the space

To help understand what Godly Play *is*, we can also take a look at what Godly Play is *not*. First, Godly Play is *not* a complete children's program. Christmas pageants, vacation Bible school, children's choirs, children's and youth groups, parent-child retreats, picnics, service opportunities and other components of a full and vibrant children's ministry are all important and are not in competition with Godly Play. What Godly Play contributes to the glorious mix of activities is the heart of the matter, the art of knowing and knowing how to use the language of the Christian people to make meaning about life and death. Children need deeply respectful experiences with scripture if they are to fully enter into its power. If we leave out the heart of the matter, we risk trivializing the Christian way of life. We also miss the profound fun of existential discovery, a kind of "fun" that keeps us truly alive!

HOW TO DO GODLY PLAY

When doing Godly Play, *be patient*. Your own teaching style, informed by the practices of Godly Play, will emerge. Even if you use another curriculum for church school, you can begin to incorporate aspects of Godly Play into your practice—beginning with elements as simple as the greeting and goodbye.

Pay careful attention to the environment you provide for children. The Godly Play environment is an "open" environment in the sense that children may make genuine choices regarding both the materials they use and the process by which they work toward shared goals. The Godly Play environment is also a "boundaried" environment in the sense that children are protected and guided to make constructive choices.

As teachers, we set nurturing boundaries for the children by managing time, space and relationships in a clear and firm way. The environment needs such limits to be the kind of safe place in which a creative encounter with God can flourish. Let's explore each of these constructive limits in greater depth.

HOW TO MANAGE TIME

AN IDEAL SESSION

In an optimum setting, a full Godly Play session takes about two hours. An ideal session has four parts, each part echoing the way most Christians organize their worship together.

OPENING: ENTERING THE SPACE AND BUILDING THE CIRCLE

The storyteller sits in the circle, waiting for the children to enter. The door person sits by the door and helps children and parents separate outside the room, and encourages the children to "slow down," mentally and physically, as they enter the room.

The storyteller helps each child sit in a specific place in the circle and greets each child warmly by name.

The storyteller, by modeling and direct instruction, helps the children get ready for the day's presentation.

HEARING THE WORD OF GOD: PRESENTATION AND RESPONSE

The storyteller first invites a child to move the hand of the Church "clock" wall hanging to the next block of color. The storyteller then presents the day's lesson. At the presentation's end, the storyteller invites the children to wonder together about the lesson. The storyteller then goes around the circle asking each child to choose work for the day. If necessary, the door person helps children get out their work, either storytelling materials or art supplies. As the children work, some might remain with the storyteller who presents another lesson to them. This smaller group is made up of those who are not able to choose work on their own yet.

SHARING THE FEAST: PREPARING THE FEAST AND SHARING IT IN HOLY LEISURE

The door person helps three children set out the napkins, food and drink for the feast—such as juice, fruit or cookies—for children to share. Children take turns saying prayers, whether silently or aloud, until the last prayer is said by the storyteller. The children and storyteller share the feast, then clean things up and put the waste in the trash.

DISMISSAL: SAYING GOODBYE AND LEAVING THE SPACE

The children get ready to say goodbye. The door person calls each child by name to say goodbye to the storyteller. The storyteller holds out hands, letting the child make the decision to hug, hold hands or not touch at all. The storyteller says goodbye and reflects on the pleasure of having the child in this community.

In an optimum setting, the opening, presentation of the lesson and wondering aloud together about the lesson might take about half an hour. The children's response to the lesson through art, retelling and other work might take about an hour. The preparation for the feast, the feast, and saying goodbye might take another half an hour.

IF YOU ONLY HAVE THE FAMOUS FORTY-FIVE MINUTE "HOUR"

You may have a limited time for your sessions—as little as forty-five minutes instead of two hours. With a forty-five minute session, you have several choices:

FOCUS ON THE FEAST

Sometimes children take especially long to get ready. If you need a full fifteen minutes to build the circle, you can move directly to the feast, leaving time for a leisurely goodbye. You will not shortchange the children. The quality of time and relationships that the children experience within the space is the most important lesson presented in a session of Godly Play.

FOCUS ON THE WORD

Most often, you will have time for a single presentation, including time for the children and you to respond to the lesson by wondering together. Finish with the feast and then the goodbye ritual. Because the children will have no time to make a work response, we suggest that every three or four sessions, you omit any presentation and focus on the work instead (see directly below).

FOCUS ON THE WORK

If you must pass from the presentation directly to the feast, then every three or four sessions, substitute a work session for a presentation. First build the circle. Then, without making a presentation, help children choose their work for the day. Allow enough time at the end of the session to share the feast and say goodbye.

HOW TO MANAGE SPACE

GETTING STARTED

We strongly recommend a thorough reading of *The Complete Guide to Godly Play, Volume 1: How to Lead Godly Play Lessons.*

To start, focus on the relationships and actions that are essential to Godly Play, rather than on the materials needed in a fully equipped Godly Play space. We know that not every parish can allocate generous funds for Christian education. We believe Godly Play is worth beginning with the simplest of resources. Without any materials at all, two teachers can make a Godly Play space that greets the children, shares a feast and blesses them goodbye each week.

When Jerome Berryman and his wife Thea began teaching, he used shelving made from boards and cinder blocks, and the first lesson was the parable of the Good Shepherd, cut from construction paper and placed in a shoe box he had spray-painted gold.

Over that first year, the Berrymans filled the shelves with additional homemade lesson materials. When more time and money became available, he upgraded those materials to ones cut from foam core. Now his research room is fully equipped with the full range of beautiful and lasting Godly Play materials: parable boxes, Noah's ark, a desert box filled with sand and more. (These materials are now available for purchase at *www.morehouseeducation.org.*) All of these riches are wonderful gifts to the children who spend time there, but the *start* of a successful Godly Play environment is the nurturing of appropriate relationships in a safe space.

MATERIALS FOR GODLY PLAY VOLUME 7

MATERIALS FOR THE PRESENTATIONS

Each lesson details the materials needed in a section titled "Notes on the Materials."
Here is a list of all suggested materials for these enrichment presentations:

- *Lesson 1: Introduction to the Communion of Saints*
  — rug
  — small basket filled with saint figures, one for each month of the year (Take from the tray for Lesson 2, *Vol. 7*)
  — "Circle of the Church Year" from the Focal shelf (Wooden Puzzle used for Lesson 1, *Vol. 2*)

- *Lesson 2: Expanded Introduction to the Communion of Saints*
  — "Circle of the Church Year" (Big felt "Circle of the Church Year" that hangs on the wall)
  — tray for materials (large enough to hold the following materials)
    - small basket filled with saint figures, one for each month of the year
    - small basket filled with flags of the countries for each saint figure
    - a map of the world
    - a time line of explorers including the saints featured in this volume.
    - "Control" that lists the saints, the country they are from and a picture of the flag
    - "Control" for the time line (a smaller time line indicating when the saints lived)

- *Lesson 3: St. Thomas Aquinas (remembered Jan. 28, died in 1274)*
  — tray
  — green cloth underlay
  — St. Thomas saint booklet
  — two miniature books entitled *Aristotle* and *The Bible*
  — ox
  — some straw

- *Lesson 4: "St." Valentine (remembered Feb. 14, died about 270)*
  — tray
  — green cloth underlay (sometimes purple as Valentine's day can fall during the season of Lent)
  — "St." Valentine saint booklet
  — small mortar and pestle
  — silk crocus
  — scroll

- *Lesson 5: St. Patrick (remembered March 17, died in 461)*
  — tray
  — purple cloth underlay
  — St. Patrick saint booklet
  — boat
  — shepherd's staff
  — three leaf clover

- *Lesson 6: St. Catherine of Siena (remembered April 29, died in 1380)*
  — tray
  — white cloth underlay
  — St. Catherine saint booklet
  — lily
  — letter
  — bridge

- *Lesson 7: St. Julian of Norwich (remembered May 8, died about 1417)*
  — tray
  — white cloth underlay
  — St. Julian saint booklet
  — little stone building with a window in it
  — hazelnut
  — wooden plaque with the words: "All shall be well, and all shall be well, and all manner of things shall be well."

- *Lesson 8: St. Columba (remembered June 9, died in 597)*
  — tray
  — green cloth underlay
  — St. Columba saint booklet
  — dove
  — illuminated manuscript page
  — photo of Iona

- *Lesson 9: St. Elizabeth of Portugal (remembered July 4, died in 1336)*
  — tray
  — green cloth underlay
  — St. Elizabeth saint booklet
  — small bunch of red silk roses
  — donkey
  — pine tree

- *Lesson 10: St. Augustine of Hippo (remembered Aug. 28, died in 430)*
  — tray
  — green cloth underlay
  — St. Augustine saint booklet
  — pear
  — three small felt circles (white)
  — piece of cloth with a tear in it

- *Lesson 11: Mother Teresa of Calcutta (died Sept. 5, 1997)*
  — tray
  — green cloth underlay
  — Mother Teresa of Calcutta saint booklet
  — bowl & small piece of cloth
  — sari like the one she wore
  — wooden plaque that reads "Peace" and also has an image of a dove.

- *Lesson 12: St. Teresa of Avila (remembered Oct. 15, died in 1582)*
  — tray
  — green cloth underlay
  — St. Teresa of Avila saint booklet
  — bed
  — donkey
  — piece of crystal

- *Lesson 13: St. Margaret of Scotland (remembered Nov. 16, died in 1093)*
  — tray
  — green cloth underlay
  — St. Margaret saint booklet
  — piece of tapestry
  — miniature church
  — some coins

- *Lesson 14: St. Nicholas, Bishop of Myra (remembered Dec. 6, died about 343)*
  — tray
  — purple cloth underlay
  — St. Nicholas saint booklet
  — statue of the Christ Child in the manger
  — bishop's miter
  — wrapped present

- *Lesson 15: The Story of the Child's Own Saint (See script.)*

- *Lesson 16: The Story of the Child's Own Life (See script.)*

MATERIALS FOR CHILDREN'S WORK

Gather art supplies that the children can use to make their responses. These materials are kept on the art shelves. We suggest:

- paper
- painting trays
- watercolor
- paints and brushes
- drawing boards
- crayons, pencils and markers
- boards for modeling clay
- clay rolled into small balls in airtight containers

MATERIALS FOR THE FEAST

- napkins
- serving basket
- cups
- tray
- pitcher

MATERIALS FOR CLEANUP

Gather cleaning materials that the children can use to clean up after their work and use to care for their environment. We suggest:

- paper towels
- feather duster
- brush and dustpan
- cleaning cloths
- spray bottles with water
- trash can with liner

HOW TO ARRANGE MATERIALS

The materials are arranged on the shelves to communicate visually and silently the language system of the Christian faith: our sacred stories, parables and our liturgical actions. Main presentations (*Volumes 2, 3, & 4*) are generally kept on the top shelves.

Enrichment presentations are kept on the second and third shelves. When room permits, supplemental materials can be gathered such as books, maps or other resources. Separate shelves hold supplies for art, cleanup and the feast. A shelf for children's work in progress is also very important.

What follows is a basic map of a Godly Play Room. The enrichment presentations in *Volume 7* will go on the shelf devoted to the Mystery of Pentecost. Within each enrichment presentation you will find a drawing of each shelf with the location of the presentation clearly marked.

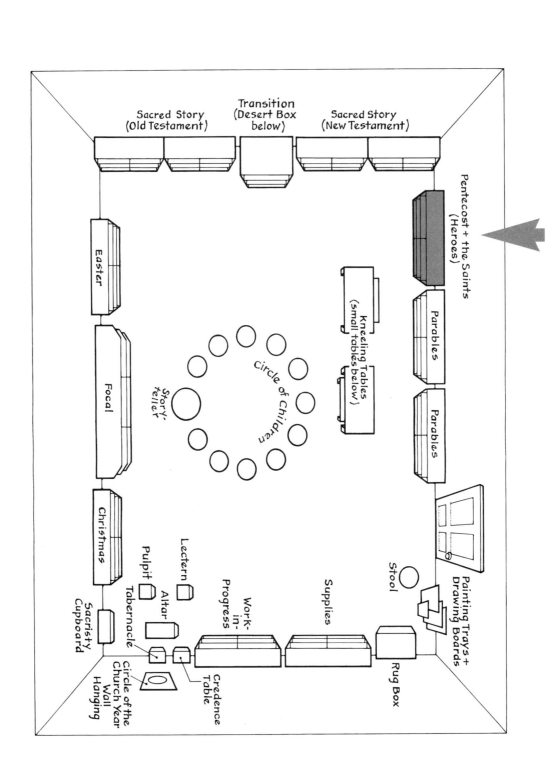

Sacred Story (Old Testament)

Transition (Desert Box below)

Sacred Story (New Testament)

Pentecost + the Saints (Heroes)

Easter

Parables

Focal

Kneeling Tables (small tables below)

Parables

Story-teller

Circle of Children

Christmas

Pulpit

Lectern

Work-in-Progress

Supplies

Stool

Painting Trays + Drawing Boards

Altar

Tabernacle

Sacristy Cupboard

Circle of the Church Year Wall Hanging

Credence Table

Rug Box

WHERE TO FIND MATERIALS

HOW TO MANAGE RELATIONSHIPS

THE TWO TEACHING ROLES: DOOR PERSON AND STORYTELLER

Each teaching role fosters respect for the children and the Godly Play space. For example, parents are left at the threshold of the Godly Play space and teachers remain at the children's eye level. Both practices keep the room child-centered, instead of adult-centered.

Similarly when the storyteller presents a lesson, his or her eyes are kept focused on the materials of the lesson—not the children. Instead of being encouraged to respond to a teacher, the children are invited, by the storyteller's eyes, to enter the story and respond to its deep meaning with God. When the wondering begins eye contact with the children is made, because the community of the circle is interpreting together what they have just experienced.

In a typical Sunday morning session, only two adults will be present in the Godly Play space; the door person and the storyteller. These are their respective tasks during typical session:

DOOR PERSON	STORYTELLER
Check the shelves, especially the supply shelves and art shelves.	Check the material to be presented that day.
Get out the roll book, review notes and get ready to greet the children and parents.	Get seated on the floor in the circle and prepare to greet the children.
Slow down the children coming into the room. You may need to take and put aside toys, books and other distracting objects. Help them to get ready. Take the roll or have the older children check themselves in.	Guide the children to places in the circle where they will best be able to attend to the lesson. Visit quietly until it is time to begin and all are ready.
Close the door when it is time. Be ready to work with latecomers and children who come to you from the circle.	Present the lesson. Model how to "enter" the material.
Avoid casual eye contact with the storyteller to help prevent the adults in the room from turning the children into objects, talking down to them, or manipulating them.	Draw the children into the lesson by your introduction. Bring your gaze down to focus on the material when you begin the actual lesson. Look up when the wondering begins.

DOOR PERSON

When the children choose their work, they may need help setting up artwork and getting materials from the shelves for work on a lesson, either alone or in a group especially if they are new.

Stay in your chair unless children need your help. Do not intrude on the community of children. Stay at the eye level of the children whenever possible, as if there is a glass ceiling in the room at the level of the taller children.

Help the children put their work away, and also help the children who are getting ready to lay out the feast.

Sit quietly in your chair. Be sure that the trash can has a liner in it.

Greet the parents and begin to call the names of the children who are ready and whose parents are there.

If a child starts for the door without saying goodbye to the storyteller, remind him or her to return to the storyteller to say goodbye.

STORYTELLER

After the lesson and wondering, go around the circle, dismissing each child to begin his or her work, one at a time. Each child chooses what to do. Go quickly around the circle the first time, returning to the children who did not decide. Go around the circle for decisions until only a few are left. These children may be new or for some other reason cannot make a choice. Present a lesson to these children.

Remain seated in the circle unless children need help with the lessons they have gotten out. You may need to help with art materials. Keep yourself at the children's eye level as you help.

When it is time for the feast, go to the light switch and turn it off. Ask the children to put their work away and come back to the circle for the feast. Turn the light back on. Go to the circle to anchor it as the children finish their work and return.

Ask for prayers, but do not pressure. After the feast, show the children how to put their things away in the trash.

Help the children get ready to have their names called.

As the children's names are called, they come to you. Hold out your hands. Children can take your hands, give a hug, or keep their distance, as they like. Tell them quietly and privately how glad you were to see them and describe the work they did that day. Invite them to come back when they can.

DOOR PERSON

Remember to give back anything that may have been taken at the beginning of class.

When the children are gone, check and clean the art and supply shelves.

Sit quietly and contemplate the session as a whole.

Evaluate, make notes and discuss the session with your co-teacher.

STORYTELLER

Take time to enjoy saying goodbye, with all the warmth of a blessing for each child.

When all are gone, check the material shelves and clean.

Sit quietly and contemplate the session as a whole.

Evaluate, make notes and discuss the session with your co-teacher.

HOW OTHERS CAN HELP

Other adults who want to support the work of a Godly Play space can contribute by:
- taking turns providing festive and healthy food for the children to share during their feasts
- keeping the art and supply shelves replenished with fresh materials
- using their creative skills to make materials for Godly Play presentations

HOW TO RESPOND EFFECTIVELY TO DISRUPTIONS IN THE CIRCLE

You always want to model the behavior you expect in the circle. Keep focused on the lesson and respectful of everyone in the circle. If a disruption occurs, you deal with that disruption in such a way that you still show continual respect for everyone in the circle—including the child who is having trouble that day. You also keep the lesson in mind, returning to complete focus on the lesson as quickly as possible.

As you respond to misbehavior keep a neutral tone in your voice. Remember, too, that our goal is to help the child move himself or herself toward more appropriate behavior. At the first level of interruption, you might simply raise your eyes from the material. You look up, but not directly at the child, while saying, "We need to get ready again. Watch. This is how we get ready." Model the way to get ready and begin again the presentation where you left off.

If the interruption continues or increases, address the child directly. "No, that's not fair. Look at all these children who are listening. They are ready. You need to be ready, too. Let's try again. Good. That's the way."

If the interruption still continues or increases, ask the child to sit by the door person. Don't think of this as a punishment or as an exclusion from the story: some children *want* to sit by the door person for their own reasons. Continue to keep a neutral tone of voice as you say, "Please go and sit by the door. It will be easier for you to be ready there. You can see and hear. The lesson is still for you."

The goal is for the child to take himself or herself to the door when needed. If the child is having trouble, or says, "No!", you can say, "May I help you?" Only if necessary do you gently pick up the child or, in some similar way, help him or her move across the room to sit on the floor by the door person.

EARLY, MIDDLE, AND LATE CHILDHOOD

When someone says or writes the word "child" or "childhood" something interesting happens to the listener or reader. A projection of a child's image into the ambiguity of such words will take place. You will select a representative from early, middle, or late childhood and, perhaps, even a particular child from your memory to give specific meaning to the general term. This can create miscommunication.

Let's agree that when we talk about children we specify whether we are talking about *early*, *middle*, or *late* childhood. Let's further agree that we will give approximate age spans for these three great developmental periods as follows: 3-6, 6-9 and 9-12.

The age grouping of 3-6, 6-9 and 9-12 comes from Montessori. She wrote before the vast amount of work done in developmental psychology that we have available today. Montessori was not just writing about developmental psychology, as for example was Piaget's focus. She was conscious of and interested in cognitive development, like Piaget was, but she was primarily thinking about what age groups would be best for children in actual classrooms. These groups are also good for Godly Play communities. In small churches you might have a single group from 3-12 and then divide it into two and then three groups as the community of children grows. In this way the older children can help the younger ones make good choices by their example as well as what they say to them as their friends and leaders.

In Godly Play the children in *early* childhood are mostly interested in how the class works. How do you come into the room? How do you sit in a circle and listen? How do you get the educational materials from the shelf? How do you go and get your art materials? How do you put things away? How do you have a feast? How do you leave the room? The primary thing that is learned, however, is to love the materials and to be at play in the wondering with the other children about what the presentations mean. If one has taught, mostly by authentic showing, how to love the language of the Christian People, then, something amazing and huge has happened in itself. It is the basis on which *middle* and *late* childhood Godly Play is built.

In *middle* childhood the children who are experienced with Godly Play are now free to work smoothly in the classroom. They know many of the lessons with their senses, even if they cannot yet articulate what they are about with words. A foundation has been laid with their body knowing. In *middle* childhood the emphasis is on speaking and reading. The reading, however, may still be at the word reading level and not yet on the paragraph-reading level. Children are often still not fully at ease with the printed page. This is why for example the Parable Synthesis Lessons (Parable Syntheses 1, Parable Synthesis 2, and Parable Synthesis 3 on pages 132-152 in *Volume 3*) are not presented until *late* childhood. These lessons require too much reading. Before children begin to rely on their eyes to understand the language of the Christian People we like for them to have deep knowledge of this language that is based on their senses as well as their minds. What is most interesting about *middle* childhood is that the children's wondering becomes verbally richer.

When presenting stories to children at any stage it is important for the adult mentor/guide to be authentic. This becomes even more of a necessity when working with children in *late* childhood. Children in *late* childhood also require teachers who are very experienced with all of the stories on the shelves. It is not possible to predict what direction the children will go in their wondering and work, so a teacher needs to be ready to go just about anywhere with them. This is difficult for an inexperienced teacher. Children have also become savvy school-goers, and will be more anxious to know what the "correct" answer is. The energy required to help the circle be comfortable in the questions and to discover their own answers with God and the community of children is enormous.

In *late* childhood the ability to be at ease with reading paragraphs and books allows the children to take books from the shelves of the Godly Play environment and not only look at the pictures but to read them. Sometimes, however, this is not to their advantage. Some children will curl up with a book and not be as aware of the community of children swirling around them. They can also use the reading as a defense against the emotional involvement with the sacred stories, the parables, the liturgical action materials, or be sensitive to God's presence in the silent spaces between words. While an adult guide might want to move children in *middle* childhood towards reading, in *late* childhood the mentor might want to move the older children back towards the materials so they can once again put their hands on this powerful language.

If you would like to read more about the theological and educational foundations for Godly Play there are concise articles by Jerome W. Berryman in the *Sewanee Theological Review*. (*Volume 48: Volume 1, Christmas 2004* and *Volume 48:4, Michaelmas 2005*.)

HOW TO SUPPORT THE CHILDREN'S "WORK" (DEEP PLAY)

Show respect for the children's work in two key ways: through the environment in which the children work and through the language you use—and do *not* use—in talking about their work. Let's explore each of these.

USING THE ENVIRONMENT

A Godly Play environment is structured to support children's work in four ways:

- First, it makes materials inviting and available by keeping the room open, clean and well-organized. A useful phrase for a Godly Play room is, "This material is for you. You can touch this and work with this when you want to. If you haven't had the lesson, ask one of the other children or the storyteller to show it to you." Children walking into a Godly Play classroom take delight at all the fascinating materials calling out to them. These materials say, "This room is for you."

- Second, it encourages responsible stewardship of the shared materials by helping children learn to take care of the room themselves. When something spills, we could quickly wipe it up ourselves, of course. Instead, by helping children learn to take care of their own spills, we communicate to them the respect we have for their own problem-solving capabilities. At the end of work time, each child learns to put away materials carefully. In fact, some children may want to choose cleaning work —dusting or watering plants—for their response time.

- Third, it provides a respectful place for children's work by reserving space in the room for ongoing or finished projects. When a child is still working on a project at the end of work time, reassure him or her by saying, "This project will be here for you next week. You can take as many weeks as you need to finish it. We never lose work in a Godly Play room." Sometimes children want to give a finished piece of work to the room. Sometimes children want to take either finished or unfinished work home. These choices are theirs to make, and ours to respect.

- Fourth, it sets a leisurely *pace* that allows children to engage deeply in their chosen responses. This is why it's better to do no more than build the circle, share a feast and lovingly say goodbye when we are pressed for time rather than rush through a story and the time of the art response. When we tell a story, we want to allow enough time for leisurely wondering together. When we provide work time, we want to allow enough time for children to become deeply engaged in their work. In their wondering or their work, children may be dealing with deep issues—issues of life and death. Provide them a nourishing *space* filled with safe time for this profound work.

USING LANGUAGE

You can also support children with the language you use:

- Choose *"open" responses*. We choose "open" responses when we simply describe what we see, rather than evaluate the children or their work. Open responses invite children's interaction, but mentors also need to respect children's choices to simply keep working in silence, too. *Examples:*
  — "Hm. Lots of red."
  — "This is big work. The paint goes all the way from here to there."
  — "This clay is so smooth. Look how it curves here."

- Avoid *evaluative responses*. Evaluative responses shift the child's focus from his or her work to your praise. In a Godly Play classroom, we want to allow children the freedom to work on what matters most to them, not for the reward of our praise. *Examples to use sparingly*:
  — "You're a wonderful painter."
  — "This is a great picture."
  — "I'm so pleased with what you did."

- Choose *empowering responses*, which emphasize each child's ability to make choices, solve problems and articulate needs. In a Godly Play classroom, frequently heard phrases are, "That's the way. You can do this." We encourage children to choose their own work, get the materials out carefully, and clean up their work areas when they are done. When a child spills something, respond with, "That's no problem. Do you know where the cleanup supplies are kept?" If a child needs help, show where the supplies are kept or how to wring out a sponge. When helping, the aim is to restore ownership of the problem or situation to the child as soon as possible.

- Stay alert to the children's *needs* during work and cleanup time. The door person's role is especially important as children get out and put away their work. By staying alert to the children's choices in the circle, the door person can know for example when to help a new child learn the routine for using clay, when a child might need help moving the desert box, or when a child might need support in putting material away or cleaning up after painting.

MORE INFORMATION ON GODLY PLAY

The Complete Guide to Godly Play, Volumes 1-8 by Jerome Berryman are available from Morehouse Education Resources. *Volume 1: How to Lead Godly Play Lessons* is the essential handbook for using Godly Play in church school or a wide variety of alternative settings. *Volumes 2-4* present complete presentations for Fall, Winter and Spring. *Volumes 6-8* contain a series of enrichment lessons to be integrated with *Volumes 2, 3, and 4. Volume 5* includes the wisdom of Godly Play trainers.

The *Godly Play Foundation* is the nonprofit organization that sponsors ongoing research, training, development of materials, accreditation programs, the development of a theology of childhood, and supports high-quality Godly Play practice around the world.

The *Godly Play Foundation* is an ecumenical and parish-based organization with centers of excellence in this country and around the world. For locations of these centers please visit our Web site at *www.godlyplay.org*

The *Foundation* maintains a schedule of training and speaking events related to Godly Play, and a list of trainers available throughout this and other countries for help in establishing Godly Play programs. For more information, contact:

Godly Play Foundation
Church of Our Savior
535 West Roses Road
San Gabriel, CA 91775
626 282-3066
www.godlyplay.org
center@godlyplay.org

Although you can make your own materials, Morehouse Education Resources now supplies the beautiful and lasting materials approved by the Godly Play Foundation especially for use in a Godly Play classroom. For more information or to place an order, contact:

Morehouse Education Resources
4775 Linglestown Road
Harrisburg, PA 17112
1-800-242-1918
fax: 1-717-541-8136
www.morehouseeducation.org

LESSON 1
INTRODUCTION TO THE COMMUNION OF SAINTS

LESSON NOTES

FOCUS: THE CHILD IS INVITED TO DISCOVER HOW HE OR SHE IS PART OF THE LARGER STORY OF THE COMMUNION OF SAINTS.

THE MATERIAL

- LOCATION: THE MYSTERY OF PENTECOST SHELF, TOP SHELF, TO THE RIGHT OF "THE MYSTERY OF PENTECOST" (VOL. 4)
- PIECES: BASKET OF SAINT FIGURES, WOODEN "CIRCLE OF THE CHURCH YEAR" (FROM THE FOCAL SHELF)
- UNDERLAY: A RUG (FROM THE BOX OF RUGS IN THE CLASSROOM USED BY THE CHILDREN DURING WORK-TIME)

BACKGROUND

Every part of the Christian tradition has its special people who are looked up to and respected as examples of what each denomination or group best exemplifies. These heroes are called by different names. The classic term used to identify such people is to call them *saints,* which is the term we use here.

We realize that this term, *saints*, may be strange or even objectionable to some. Please don't let this terminology problem get in the way of enjoying the stories of the remarkable people included in this volume. You may want to add the special people from your denomination to those celebrated here and we encourage that. You may also want to add your own special people and Lessons 15 and 16 in this volume are provided for you and the children to do just that.

The most important point about the lessons in this volume is to develop a larger sense of saints—living and dead, known and unknown—of which you are one. Thanks be to God for you and for this community that can be so life-giving in times of celebration and sadness.

NOTES ON THE MATERIAL

This lesson is told on a rug from the box of rugs in the classroom used by the children during work-time. This lesson shares a tray with Lesson 2 (*Vol. 7*), an expanded introduction to the communion of saints. The tray sits on the top shelf of the Mystery of Pentecost shelf, to the right of "The Mystery of Pentecost" (*Vol. 4*). The tray holds a small basket containing the twelve figures needed for this lesson and other materials used for Lesson 2 (*Vol. 7*). You will also use the wooden "Circle of the Church Year" (*Vol. 2*) material that sits on the Focal shelf.

SPECIAL NOTES

This lesson serves as an introduction to the communion of saints' for children new to Godly Play. It could be told on All Saints' Day (celebrated in early November), after telling "The Mystery of Pentecost" (*Vol. 4*), or anytime during the season of Easter. There is a saint for each month of the secular calendar.

A NOTE ABOUT DATES FOR THE SAINTS

There is scholarly debate about the dates for the lives of many saints. We have had to make decisions about these dates for pedagogical reasons. We hope the children will continue to learn more about the saints all their life long, including their dates. The basis for the dates used in this volume is how they are remembered liturgically. This has been established by custom in the Roman Catholic, Anglican, and other traditions. We usually follow the dates that are found in the Episcopal publication called *Lesser Feasts and Fasts, 2006*. This book is also a reference for remembering saints for most days in the year and for children (and adults) to continue to learn more about the saints, using this liturgical orientation.

You can order this book at *www.morehouseeducation.org* or by calling: 1-800-242-1918.

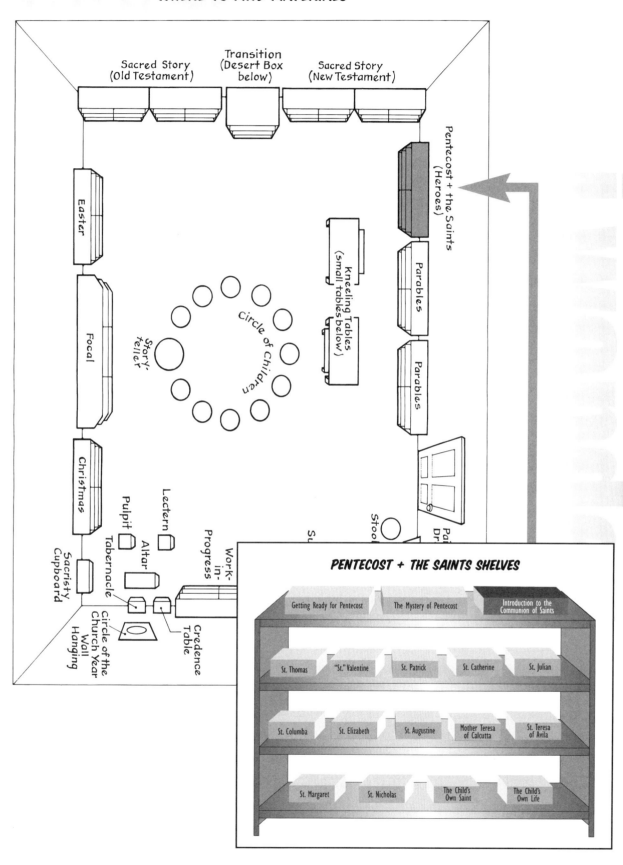

Sacred Story (Old Testament)

Transition (Desert Box below)

Sacred Story (New Testament)

Pentecost + the Saints (Heroes)

Easter

Focal

Christmas

Story-teller

Circle of Children

Kneeling Tables (small tables below)

Parables

Parables

Sacristy Cupboard

Tabernacle

Pulpit

Altar

Lectern

Work-in-Progress

Circle of the Church Year Wall Hanging

Credence Table

Stool

PENTECOST + THE SAINTS SHELVES

Getting Ready for Pentecost

The Mystery of Pentecost

Introduction to the Communion of Saints

St. Thomas

"St." Valentine

St. Patrick

St. Catherine

St. Julian

St. Columba

St. Elizabeth

St. Augustine

Mother Teresa of Calcutta

St. Teresa of Avila

St. Margaret

St. Nicholas

The Child's Own Saint

The Child's Own Life

MOVEMENTS	WORDS
Move with deliberation to the box or basket of work rugs. Return to your spot in the circle and unroll the rug in front of you.	Watch. Watch where I go. First we need a rug.
Move with deliberation to the shelf where the material waits.	Now let's see. What else do we need?
Pick up the basket of saint figures from the tray containing the materials for both Lesson 1 (Vol. 7) and Lesson 2 (Vol. 7) and return to your spot. Place the basket of saint figures on the rug and say:	We need one more thing.
Turn around and get the wooden "Circle of the Church Year" (Vol. 2) from the Focal shelf and place it on the rug to the left of the basket of saints' (Storyteller's perspective).	Now we have everything we need.
Look around and wait for children to settle.	Look around our circle. You see a circle of friends.
As you speak about the circle gesture to the children seated on the floor with you.	Did you know that there are more people in this circle than you can see? They come to join us from the whole story of the Christian people.

Look around the room. You can see lessons about some of these people, but there are many more.

Many of these people the church remembers as saints. They are special friends, who loved God and people very well. |
| Hold up the basket of saint figures then set it down again and pause. | Today we will remember just twelve of them. Six boys and six girls. And here they are. |
| Pick up the Circle of the Church Year and then put it down again. | We don't know exactly where the months are in this circle, but there is a remarkable person for each month. |
| Pick up each saint figure beginning with St. Thomas and place them facing inward on the circle next to the time in our year when we remember that saint. | Here is St. Thomas, who thought for God.

Here is "St." Valentine, who loved for God. |

MOVEMENTS

Note: The Circle of the Church Year does not correspond exactly with the secular calendar, but we know that January is right after Christmas, and so on. Place Thomas right after Christmas and the saints that follow about four blocks apart.

WORDS

Here is St. Patrick, who traveled for God.

Here is St. Catherine of Siena, who showed people how to be fair for God.

Here is St. Julian of Norwich, who was quiet and wise for God.

Here is St. Columba of Scotland, who loved books and people for God.

Here is St. Elizabeth of Portugal, who was peaceful and made peace for God.

Here is St. Augustine, who was restless and found rest in God.

Here is Mother Teresa of Calcutta, who cared for the sick and poor for God.

Here is St. Teresa of Avila, who was strict but laughed for God.

Here is St. Margaret of Scotland, who cared for her own children and the people of her country for God.

Here is St. Nicholas, who gave gifts for God.

They all prayed and came close to God. And they all did amazing things.

COMPLETE LAYOUT OF THE COMMUNION OF SAINTS

MOVEMENTS	WORDS
Point to the sequence around the "Circle of the Church Year."	See, there is one for each month.
As the children answer you can show them which saint is remembered during the month they were born.	Now, what month were you born in?
	There is a saint close to each one of your birthdays. That's your special friend.
Pause. Look around the circle once again and begin the wondering.	I wonder what part of this circle of saints you like best?
	I wonder what part of this circle is most important?
	I wonder what part is especially about you?
	I wonder if there is any part of this circle that we could leave out and still have everyone we need?
When the wondering winds down, model how to put the material away. Start by placing the saint figures in their basket. Bring that back to its spot on the shelf. Put the "Circle of the Church Year" back on the Focal shelf. Roll up the rug and return it to the rug basket. Name each item as you put it away.	Here are the saints—one for each month. They go back on the Pentecost shelf.
	Here is the "Circle of the Church Year."
	And here is the rug. Remember we roll up the rugs, and they go back in the basket.
Return to your spot in the circle and begin to help the children decide on and move to their work.	Now, I wonder what you'd like to make your work today?

LESSON 2

EXPANDED INTRODUCTION TO THE COMMUNION OF SAINTS

LESSON NOTES

FOCUS: THE CHILD'S PARTICIPATION IN THE COMMUNION OF SAINTS IS GIVEN MORE DETAIL AND HISTORICAL CONTEXT.

THE MATERIAL

- LOCATION: THE MYSTERY OF PENTECOST SHELF, TOP SHELF, TO THE RIGHT OF "THE MYSTERY OF PENTECOST" (VOL. 4)

- PIECES: FELT "CIRCLE OF THE CHURCH YEAR" (THE ONE THAT HANGS ON THE WALL OF THE CLASSROOM), TRAY CONTAINING THE BASKET OF SAINT FIGURES, MAP OF THE WORLD, BASKET CONTAINING THE FLAGS FROM THE COUNTRIES OF THE DIFFERENT SAINTS, TIME LINE OF EXPLORERS, "CONTROL" THAT LISTS THE SAINTS, THE COUNTRY THEY ARE FROM AND A PICTURE OF THE FLAG, "CONTROL" FOR THE TIME LINE (A SMALLER TIME LINE INDICATING WHEN THE SAINTS LIVED)

- UNDERLAY: THE FELT "CIRCLE OF THE CHURCH YEAR" WILL SERVE AS AN UNDERLAY FOR THIS LESSON.

BACKGROUND

Every part of the Christian tradition has its special people that are looked up to and respected as examples of what each denomination or group best exemplifies. These heroes are called by different names. The classic term used to identify such people is to call them *saints*, which is the term we use here.

We realize that this term, *saints*, may be strange or even objectionable to some. Please don't let this terminology problem get in the way of enjoying the stories of the remarkable people included in this volume. You may want to add the special people from your denomination to those celebrated here and we encourage that. You may also want to add your own special people and Lessons 15 and 16 in this volume are provided for you and the children to do just that.

We have chosen to place these saints among the great explorers throughout history, because of their adventurous and often creative spirits. Like the great explorers, they often ventured into new places, both literally and figuratively.

The most important point about the lessons in this volume is to develop a larger sense of saints—living and dead, known and unknown—of which you are one. Thanks be to God for you and for this community that can be so life giving in times of celebration and sadness.

NOTES ON THE MATERIAL

This lesson is told on the felt "Circle of the Church Year" that hangs in a Godly Play classroom. The additional materials needed for the lesson are on a tray that sits on the top shelf of the Mystery of Pentecost shelf, to the right of the "Mystery of Pentecost" lesson (*Vol. 4*) as you look at the shelf. The tray holds a small basket containing the twelve figures needed for this lesson, a map of the world, a basket containing flags for the countries of each of the saints and a time line of great explorers including the saints featured in this lesson and in this volume. Finally, the tray also holds two "controls"—one lists the saints, the country from which they come and a picture of the flag of that country; the second is a small version of the time line indicating when the saints lived. The "controls" can be used by the children and storyteller to help them remember the many details of this lesson.

SPECIAL NOTES

This lesson adds to Lesson 1 of this volume an "Introduction to the Communion of Saints." It could be told on All Saints' Day (celebrated in early November), after telling "The Mystery of Pentecost" (Lesson 13, *Vol. 4*), anytime during the season of Easter, or when children have questions about these remarkable people. There is a saint for each month of the secular calendar. This lesson is different from Lesson 1 (*Vol. 7*) in that it places each saint not only on the Calendar of the Church Year, but also where the saint was born—and on the time line when the saint lived.

This is a long lesson requiring lots of materials and movement. Depending on how long you have with the children, this might be a good week to skip the work period and move right to the feast at the end of the lesson. This also may need to be spread over several Sundays.

The "Expanded Introduction" has five parts:
• linking the "Circle of the Church Year" to the ordinary calendar
• placing a saint figure for each month
• placing the saint's flag for each month and finding his or her home on the map
• locating each saint on the time line
• introducing the material for each individual saint and how to use it

A NOTE ABOUT DATES FOR THE SAINTS

There is scholarly debate about the dates for the lives of many saints. We have had to make decisions about these dates for pedagogical reasons. We hope the children will continue to learn more about the saints all their life long, including their dates. The basis for the dates used in this volume is how they are remembered liturgically. This has been established by custom in the Roman Catholic, Anglican, and other traditions. We usually follow the dates that are found in the Episcopal publication called *Lesser Feasts and Fasts, 2006*. This book is also a reference for remembering saints for most days in the year and for children (and adults) to continue to learn more about the saints, using this liturgical orientation.

You can order this book at *www.morehouseeducation.org*
or by calling: 1-800-242-1918.

WHERE TO FIND MATERIALS

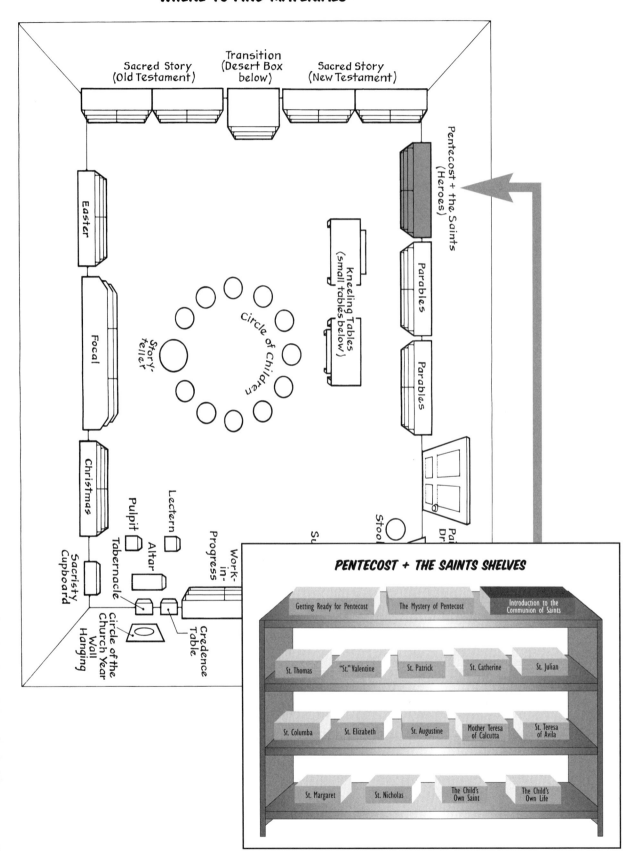

Sacred Story (Old Testament)

Transition (Desert Box below)

Sacred Story (New Testament)

Pentecost + the Saints (Heroes)

Easter

Focal

Christmas

Story-teller

Circle of Children

Kneeling Tables (small tables below)

Parables

Parables

Stool

Work-in-Progress

Lectern

Pulpit

Altar

Tabernacle

Sacristy Cupboard

Circle of the Church Year Wall Hanging

Credence Table

PENTECOST + THE SAINTS SHELVES

Getting Ready for Pentecost

The Mystery of Pentecost

Introduction to the Communion of Saints

St. Thomas

"St." Valentine

St. Patrick

St. Catherine

St. Julian

St. Columba

St. Elizabeth

St. Augustine

Mother Teresa of Calcutta

St. Teresa of Avila

St. Margaret

St. Nicholas

The Child's Own Saint

The Child's Own Life

MOVEMENTS	WORDS
Bring the large felt "Circle of the Church Year" and lay it in the middle of the circle of children.	Watch where I go….
Then get the material from the Mystery of Pentecost shelf for the communion of saints' lessons.	We need something else.
	Now we have everything we need.
As you speak about the circle, gesture to the children seated on the floor.	Look around our circle. You see a circle of friends.
	Did you know that there are more people in this circle than you can see? They come to join us from the whole story of the Christian people.
	Look around the room. You can see lessons about some of these people, but there are many more.
	Many of these people the church remembers as saints. They are special friends who loved God and people very well.
Hold up the basket of saint figures then set it down again and pause.	Today we will remember just twelve of them. Six boys and six girls. And here they are.
Indicate the "Circle" on the floor with your hand.	Here is the "Circle of the Church Year." We don't know exactly where the months are on this, but we do know that there are twelve months and the church remembers many saints for each month. We will just remember one for each month today.
Take the figure of St. Thomas from the basket and show it to the children.	I wonder if anyone in the circle has a birthday in January? We can see where January is on this circle because it is always right after Christmas. Here is one of the saints the church remembers in January, St. Thomas, who thought for God.
Show them Christmas and then place St. Thomas at the beginning of the "green time" after Christmas.	
Place "St." Valentine approximately four to six felt blocks after St. Thomas, approximating the beginning of February. If no one has a birthday in a given month, simply name the saint for that month and keep moving on.	I wonder if anyone has a birthday in February? Here is one of the saints the church remembers in February—"St." Valentine, who loved for God.

MOVEMENTS

Continue placing the saints around the calendar, approximately four to six felt blocks apart, working to space them evenly around the big circle.

Take your time. Look around the circle carefully to be sure that every child is included.

You should have reached the "purple time" of Advent by the time you get to St. Nicholas.

WORDS

Does anyone have a birthday in March? Here is one of the saints the church remembers in March—St. Patrick, who traveled for God.

Does anyone have a birthday in April? Here is one of the saints the church remembers in April—St. Catherine of Siena, who taught people how to be fair for God.

Does anyone have a birthday in May? Here is one of the saints the church remembers in May—St. Julian of Norwich, who was quiet and wise for God.

Does anyone have a birthday in June? Here is one of the saints the church remembers in June—St. Columba of Scotland, who loved books and people for God.

Does anyone have a birthday in July? Here is one of the saints the church remembers in July—St. Elizabeth of Portugal, who was peaceful and made peace for God.

Does anyone have a birthday in August? Here is one of the saints the church remembers in August—St. Augustine, who was restless and found rest in God.

Does anyone have a birthday in September? Here is someone the church remembers in September—Mother Teresa of Calcutta, who cared for the sick and poor for God.

What about October? Here is one of the saints the church remembers in October—St. Teresa of Avila, who was strict, but laughed for God

Does anyone have a birthday in November? Here is one of the saints the church remembers in November—St. Margaret of Scotland, who cared for her own children and the people of her country for God.

Now what about December? Here is one of the saints the church remembers in December—St. Nicholas, who gave gifts for God.

Now each of these saints lived in a certain place and time. You can still visit the places where they lived.

MOVEMENTS

Take the flag of Italy out of the tray for the communion of saints and put it beside Thomas. Repeat this for each of the saints as the script directs.

Take the world map from the tray and unfold it in the middle of the "Circle of the Church Year." Show the children where they are on the map and where Italy is, flying to Italy with your hand. Repeat this action for each saint as the script directs.

WORDS

St. Thomas, who thought for God, lived in Italy. Here is the flag of Italy.

Let me show you where Italy is on the map.

Here is where we are and here is where you would go to visit Italy.

"St." Valentine, who loved for God, also lived in Italy. Here is another flag of Italy.

St. Patrick, who traveled for God, lived most of his life in Ireland. Here is the flag of Ireland.

Here we are again, and here is where you would go to visit Ireland.

St. Catherine of Siena, who showed people how to be fair for God, also lived in Italy. Here is another flag of Italy.

St. Julian of Norwich, who was quiet and wise for God, lived in England. England is part of the United Kingdom. Here is the flag of the United Kingdom.

Here we are again, and here is where you would go to visit England.

St. Columba of Scotland, who loved books and people for God, lived most of his life in Scotland, which is part of the United Kingdom. Here is the flag of the United Kingdom.

Here is where you would go to visit Scotland.

St. Elizabeth of Portugal, who was peaceful and made peace for God, lived in Portugal for most of her life. Here is the flag of Portugal.

Here is where you would go to visit Portugal.

St. Augustine, who was restless and found rest in God, lived in the North of Africa in what is now Algeria. Here is the flag of Algeria.

MOVEMENTS	WORDS

Here is where you would go to visit Algeria.

Mother Teresa of Calcutta, who cared for the sick and poor for God, lived most of her life in Calcutta of India. Here is the flag of India.

Here is where you would go to visit India.

St. Teresa of Avila, who was strict, but laughed for God, lived in Spain. Here is the flag of Spain.

Here is where you would go to visit Spain.

St. Margaret of Scotland, who cared for her own children and the people of her country for God, lived most of her life in Scotland, part of the United Kingdom. Here is the flag of the United Kingdom.

Remember? Here is where Scotland is on the map.

St. Nicholas, who gave gifts for God, lived in Myra, which is now in Turkey. Here is the flag of Turkey.

Here is where you would go to visit Turkey.

Take out the "control" from the basket of flags that shows the saints, the country they are from and a picture of the flag for that country.

When you work with this yourself you can use this list (Show the control.) to help you remember where the saints lived and what their flag looks like.

Take the time line from the tray for the communion of saints and unroll it. It is bigger than the circle so you can unroll it all the way with the help of the children. When you come to the end, show them where we are on the line.

Let's find out a little more about when each of these saints lived. Look. Here is time in a line. It goes on and on. I wonder when it ends? Ah...it ended. Look, this is where we are on this line.

Be sure everyone is back in the circle as you roll the time line back up and then unroll it so it is easier to manage and fits in the center of the "Circle of the Church Year."

This time line shows when the great explorers of history lived.

MOVEMENTS

Unroll it enough to show them where Alexander the Great lived.

Take out the control for the time line (a smaller time line indicating when the saints lived) to help you place each saint at the correct point on the line.

The time line is long, so as you work with it you will need to roll up the parts that you don't need. Take your time. Let the beginning roll up as you look for the first saint (it will be Valentine) and then let it lay flat. Show the children where Thomas appears on the control, and then find him on the big time line. Point to the picture of Thomas on the time line, and then gesture to the figure of Thomas standing at his spot on the Circle of the Church Year. Do this for each saint in turn.

Each time use the control to help you. Do this in the order we remember them throughout the year: Thomas, Valentine, Patrick, Catherine of Siena, Julian of Norwich, Columba, Elizabeth of Portugal, Augustine of Hippo, Teresa of Calcutta, Teresa of Avila, Margaret of Scotland, and Nicholas.

As you locate each saint in time note those who are close in time and one or two things about each person to

WORDS

Here is one of the first great explorers, Alexander the Great. It says he lived around 334 BC—that's before Jesus Christ was born. They think he was one of the first people from Europe to travel all the way to Asia. He took his whole army with him!

The saints are also on this line. They come after Jesus was born, much later. They are on this line because they were explorers too. Sometimes they traveled to new places, or discovered new things about God and about people.

Now let me show you when St. Thomas lived. We can use this "control" to help us remember. Here he is at the year 1274 (now after Jesus' birth)—the year St. Thomas died. Let's see where he is on the big time line.

MOVEMENTS	WORDS

link them together.
Sit back and enjoy the whole lesson.

COMPLETE LAYOUT OF THE COMMUNION OF SAINTS WITH FLAGS

You then begin the wondering.

⟹ I wonder what part of this you like the best?

I wonder what part of this is the most important?

I wonder what part you are especially interested in?

I wonder if we could leave any of this out and still have all that we need?

When the wondering comes to an end you have one more thing to show the children.

⟹ Now would you like to see how to learn more about each saint? Let me show you how to do that.

Go to the Mystery of Pentecost shelf and take one of the saint lessons off to show to the children. Bring it to the circle and show the children all of the pieces.

MOVEMENTS

First take out the booklet for the saint and show the children the image of the saint on the first page. Pick up the saint figure that matches it and show the children.

Open the booklet and show the children the map and the image of the flag on the second page. Point to the matching flag and the country on the big map.

Show the children how the time lines match.

Bring the saint lesson back to the shelf.

Return to your spot and start putting away the rest of the story, modeling how all of it goes back to a special spot.

Return to your spot in the circle and begin to dismiss the children to their work if there is time. You will probably go directly to the feast and may need to do part of this lesson on following Sundays.

WORDS

Here is St. _____. Here is his/her picture. You can match it to the figure we used in this lesson.

On the second page there is a map of the world with the saint's country highlighted. There is also a picture of the flag. You can match this with the big map and the flags in the basket when you work with it on your own.

On the third page is a time line like the one in our lesson.

And on the back page is the story of the saint.

In the tray are some objects to help us remember this saint's story.

Now while I put all of this away, you can begin to think about what you would like to make your work today.

First let's put _____back on the shelf.

Here are all of the saints.

Here are their flags.

Here is the time line.

Here is the map of the world.

Let's put this all back on the shelf where it stays in our room.

And now here is the "Circle of the Church Year." It goes back to its spot on the wall.

Now what would you like to make your work today?

LESSON 3

THE STORY OF ST. THOMAS AQUINAS
(REMEMBERED JAN. 28, DIED IN 1274)

LESSON NOTES

FOCUS: ST. THOMAS THOUGHT FOR GOD.

THE MATERIAL

- LOCATION: THE MYSTERY OF PENTECOST SHELF, SECOND SHELF, UNDER GETTING READY FOR PENTECOST (VOL. 8).
- PIECES: ST. THOMAS AQUINAS BOOKLET, SAINT STAND, TWO MINIATURE BOOKS (ARISTOTLE AND THE BIBLE), AN OX, SOME STRAW
- UNDERLAY: GREEN

BACKGROUND

We remember St. Thomas on the day that he died, January 28, 1274. He was born in Italy and became a priest as a young man. He is important for his concise synthesis of Christian thought, which blended revelation and reason.

NOTES ON THE MATERIAL

St. Thomas Aquinas's story sits on a small, shallow tray about 8 inches square, with sides about two inches deep. It has a groove in the front to slide the "saint booklet" in so the children can see it when they approach the Mystery of Pentecost shelf.

The booklet is 4.25" x 5.5". The cover has an image of St. Thomas on it that matches the saint figure used in the introductory lessons on the communion of saints. The second page has a map of the world on it, with Italy, Thomas's home, highlighted and labeled. It also has an image of the flag of Italy. The third page has a time line beginning with the year 1 AD and ending with the year 2000 AD. It has an arrow indicating when Thomas lived. The rest of the book contains the story of the life of Thomas.

Behind the booklet in the tray are placed the objects used to help us remember Thomas's life: two miniature books labeled *Aristotle* and *Bible,* an ox and some straw. The underlay is a 12" square piece of green cloth and is folded on top of the objects.

ST. THOMAS AQUINAS TRAY

A NOTE ABOUT DATES FOR THE SAINTS

There is scholarly debate about the dates for the lives of many saints. We have had to make decisions about these dates for pedagogical reasons. We hope the children will continue to learn more about the saints all their life long, including their dates. The basis for the dates used in this volume is how they are remembered liturgically. This has been established by custom in the Roman Catholic, Anglican, and other traditions. We usually follow the dates that are found in the Episcopal publication called *Lesser Feasts and Fasts, 2006*. This book is also a reference for remembering saints for most days in the year and for children (and adults) to continue to learn more about the saints, using this liturgical orientation.

You can order this book at *www.morehouseeducation.org* or by calling: 1-800-242-1918.

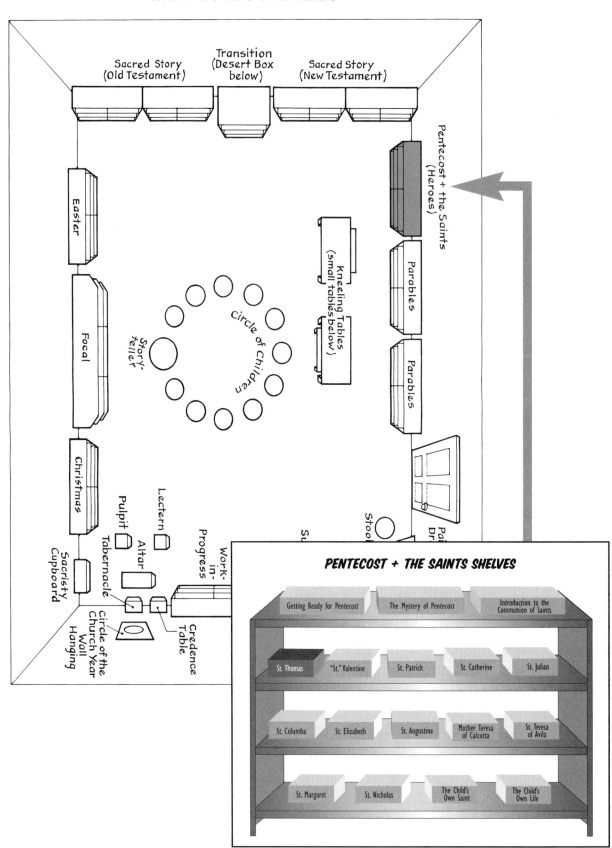

Sacred Story (Old Testament)

Transition (Desert Box below)

Sacred Story (New Testament)

Pentecost + the Saints (Heroes)

Easter

Focal

Story-teller

Circle of Children

Kneeling Tables (small tables below)

Parables

Parables

Christmas

Pulpit

Lectern

Altar

Tabernacle

Sacristy Cupboard

Circle of the Church Year Wall Hanging

Credence Table

Work-in-Progress

Stool

PENTECOST + THE SAINTS SHELVES

Getting Ready for Pentecost

The Mystery of Pentecost

Introduction to the Communion of Saints

St. Thomas

"St." Valentine

St. Patrick

St. Catherine

St. Julian

St. Columba

St. Elizabeth

St. Augustine

Mother Teresa of Calcutta

St. Teresa of Avila

St. Margaret

St. Nicholas

The Child's Own Saint

The Child's Own Life

MOVEMENTS	WORDS
Go and get the material for Thomas's story.	Watch where I go to get the lesson for today.
Unfold the green underlay in front of you and say:	This is the story of St. Thomas Aquinas. The church remembers Thomas in the time of the color green. I wonder *why* we remember Thomas? Let's see.
Take the saint booklet from the tray and place it in the center of the underlay with Thomas's image facing up and toward the children.	When little Tommaso D'Aquino was born he first lived in an old castle about halfway between Naples and Rome. He was the last of four boys and five girls born into his family.
	When he was about 5 years old his family gave him to the monastery at Monte Cassino. This was a great Benedictine monastery nearby. They thought that someday he would be the leader of the monks who lived there.
	When he was about 12 years old he went to the University of Naples, which seems strange because he wasn't very old, but he was very smart for his age.
	At the University of Naples he met Jordan of Saxony, who was a Dominican monk and a great teacher. He also began to read the books of a Greek philosopher named Aristotle.
Place one book on each side of the booklet.	All the rest of his life he had two favorite kinds of books: the Bible and those written by Aristotle.
	Finally he decided he would not become a Benedictine monk but instead became a Dominican Friar or Brother, like Jordan of Saxony.
Place the ox on the underlay.	Thomas was very bright and very quiet. His nickname was *the silent ox* because he was also huge. Some people think he was six feet six inches tall.
	One day he dropped a page of notes as he went into his room. Another student took it to his teacher, Albert the Great. After seeing the notes and after hearing his answers to the questions in a class, Albert said that this "silent ox" would be heard around the world.
	The Dominicans sent him to Paris, where the greatest University in the world was. There he began to study how to talk about God. Talking about God is called *theology*.

MOVEMENTS

WORDS

Thomas studied hard and earned a doctor of theology degree and began to write theology. Ever since he was a little boy he had had many questions about God, so he began to write his books that way. He would write a question, write all the different answers he could find, and then write what *he* thought. He asked many questions and wrote pages and pages about Aristotle, the Bible and God.

Finally when he was old, on the Feast of St. Nicholas, something happened while he was presiding at Holy Communion. For three days he was in a daze.

Put the straw on the underlay.

Finally he told a friend what he had discovered. The answers to his biggest questions about God were beyond words. He was not going to write anymore. He said that all he had written was like so much straw. Instead of writing about God now he only wanted to be close to God.

COMPLETE LAYOUT OF THE STORY OF THOMAS AQUINAS

MOVEMENTS

WORDS

When Thomas was very old the Pope sent him to a meeting in France. It was a long journey and he died on the way.

We remember Thomas because he asked questions for God. He found many answers he could write, but the most important thing he knew about God could not be put into words. He knew that by being close to God.

Guide the wondering about Thomas's life by using these wondering questions.

I wonder what parts of Thomas's story you like the best?

I wonder what part of the story is the most important?

I wonder what part of the story is about you or where you might be in the story?

I wonder if we could leave any part of the story out and still have all the story that we need?

Show the children the booklet. Point out the map of the world showing where Thomas lived, the flag of the country, the time line showing when he lived, and the story printed in the booklet to help the children know Thomas better.

Let me show you what is inside this booklet and how you can use it to find out more about Thomas.

Model how to put the lesson back on the tray and then carry it back to its spot on the shelf.

Now let me show you how to put the story away. Here is an ox to remind us about what he was called when he was a student. Here are the two books Thomas loved—Aristotle and the Bible. Here is the straw. It reminds us that Thomas said all that he wrote was like straw after he experienced God's presence in the Mass. Here is the booklet that helps us remember more about Thomas. And here is the green underlay, because we remember Thomas during the time of the green and growing Sundays during the year.

Return to your spot on the circle and begin to dismiss the children to their work.

Now I wonder what you would like to make your work today?

LESSON 4
THE STORY OF "ST." VALENTINE
(REMEMBERED FEB. 14, DIED ABOUT 270)

LESSON NOTES

FOCUS: "ST." VALENTINE LOVED FOR GOD.

THE MATERIAL

● LOCATION: THE MYSTERY OF PENTECOST SHELF, SECOND SHELF, NEXT TO ST. THOMAS

● PIECES: ST. VALENTINE BOOKLET, SAINT STAND, A SMALL MORTAR AND PESTLE, A SILK CROCUS, A SCROLL THAT HAS AN IMAGE OF A HEART AND THE WORDS, "FROM YOUR VALENTINE"

● UNDERLAY: GREEN (OR PURPLE)

BACKGROUND

Valentine was executed on February 14, 270 during one of the persecutions ordered by Emperor Claudius II Gothicus. The practice of sending love messages on February 14 originated in part from the story of Valentine's note to the jailer's blind daughter that is part of this lesson. It is also tied to the ancient Roman feast of Lupercalia, which took place on February 15. One of the customs on this occasion involved the writing of love messages by maidens. Thus, the holiday celebrated on February 14, Valentine's Day, is both a celebration of love and a commemoration of Valentine's life.

NOTES ON THE MATERIAL

"St." Valentine's story sits on a small, shallow tray about 8 inches square, with sides about two inches deep. It has a groove in the front to slide the "saint booklet" in so the children can see it when they approach the Mystery of Pentecost shelf.

The booklet is 4.25" x 5.5". The cover has an image of "St." Valentine on it that matches the saint figure used in the introductory lessons on the communion of saints. The second page has a map of the world on it, with Italy, Valentine's home, highlighted and labeled. It also has an image of the flag of Italy. The third page has a time line beginning with the year 1 AD and ending with the year 2000 A.D. It has an arrow indicating when Valentine lived. The rest of the booklet contains the story of the life of Valentine.

Behind the booklet in the tray are placed the objects used to help us remember Valentine's life: A small mortar and pestle of the kind that "St." Valentine might have used to grind up the herbs he found so he could use them as medicine, a silk crocus, and a scroll that has an image of a heart and the words, "From your Valentine." The underlay is a 12" square piece of green cloth and is folded on top of the objects. Sometimes Valentine's Day falls during the season of Lent. When that happens you can borrow a purple underlay from one of the other Lent saints when telling Valentine.

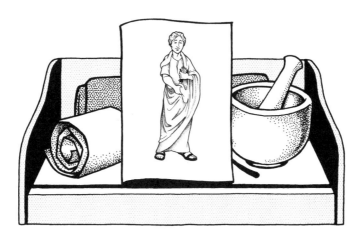

"SAINT" VALENTINE TRAY

A NOTE ABOUT DATES FOR THE SAINTS

There is scholarly debate about the dates for the lives of many saints. We have had to make decisions about these dates for pedagogical reasons. We hope the children will continue to learn more about the saints all their life long, including their dates. The basis for the dates used in this volume is how they are remembered liturgically. This has been established by custom in the Roman Catholic, Anglican, and other traditions. We usually follow the dates that are found in the Episcopal publication called *Lesser Feasts and Fasts, 2006*. This book is also a reference for remembering saints for most days in the year and for children (and adults) to continue to learn more about the saints, using this liturgical orientation.

You can order this book at *www.morehouseeducation.org* or by calling: 1-800-242-1918.

WHERE TO FIND MATERIALS

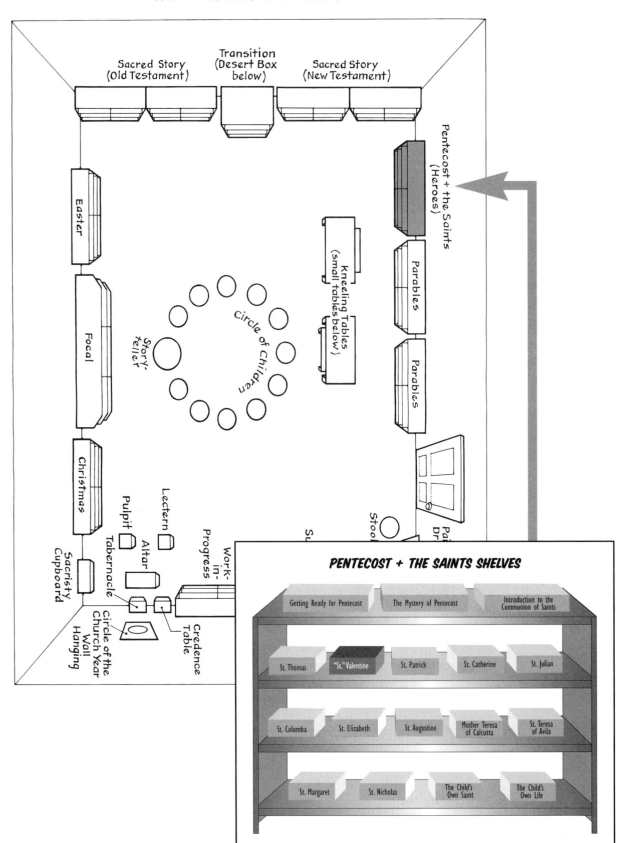

Sacred Story (Old Testament)

Transition (Desert Box below)

Sacred Story (New Testament)

Pentecost + the Saints (Heroes)

Easter

Parables

Parables

Focal

Storyteller

circle of Children

Kneeling Tables (small tables below)

Christmas

Pulpit

Lectern

Altar

Work-in-Progress

Stool

Sacristy Cupboard

Tabernacle

Circle of the Church Year Wall Hanging

Credence Table

PENTECOST + THE SAINTS SHELVES

Getting Ready for Pentecost

The Mystery of Pentecost

Introduction to the Communion of Saints

St. Thomas

"St." Valentine

St. Patrick

St. Catherine

St. Julian

St. Columba

St. Elizabeth

St. Augustine

Mother Teresa of Calcutta

St. Teresa of Avila

St. Margaret

St. Nicholas

The Child's Own Saint

The Child's Own Life

MOVEMENTS

Go and get the material for Valentine's story.

Unfold the underlay in front of you. (Sometimes Valentine's Day falls during the season of Lent. When that happens you can borrow a purple underlay from one of the other Lent saints when telling Valentine.) Say:

Take the saint booklet from the tray and place it in the center of the underlay.

Place the small mortar and pestle on the underlay to the right of the booklet.

WORDS

Watch where I go to get the lesson for today.

This is the story of "St." Valentine. The church remembers him during the time of the color green (or, during the season of Lent, a purple time). I wonder *why* we remember Valentine? Let's see.

There was once a man named Valentine who lived in ancient Rome. Not in one of the big houses of smooth, white marble but in rooms above the noisy street. He was a doctor.

In his rooms he had many things to heal people, mostly herbs that he picked in the fields outside the city. He used something like this to grind up the herbs so he could use them for medicine. When people came to see him, sometimes they didn't have money to pay him so he would accept something they had made—a pair of sandals or some warm bread—instead.

Not everyone knew that he was also a priest. That had to be kept a secret, because in those days it was against the law to be a Christian. Whenever anything bad happened in the city they would blame the Christians and put them in jail, or kill them.

So when Valentine prayed he did so quietly after closing his door.

One day an old man and a little girl came to his home. She could not see. She was the old man's daughter. He took care of the prisoners in the big jail in Rome.

Valentine knew that it would be hard to cure her because she had been born blind. But he loved to talk to her and he put something cool and wet on her eyes to make them feel better.

When the old man wanted to pay Valentine said, "No, I want to give this to your daughter."

At night when he prayed for his patients he prayed the most for the little girl.

Valentine and the little girl became good friends. Sometimes when her father was busy at the jail, Valentine and the little girl would go into the fields to pick the herbs he used to heal people.

MOVEMENTS	WORDS
Take the crocus from the tray and place it on the underlay beside the booklet.	The little girl loved to pick the first flowers to bloom in Rome after winter; the little crocuses. She gave them to her father.

One time Valentine heard a noise outside his door. He hoped it was the little girl, but instead there was a terrible crash. The Roman soldiers broke into his home and took him away. They had found out that he was a Christian and they took him to the very jail where the little girl's father was the jailer.

The old man could hardly believe his eyes when Valentine was brought into the jail. He didn't know what to do.

A few days later the soldiers came to take Valentine away. Before he left he asked for a pen and some ink and something to write on. The jailer hurried away to find it. When he came back, Valentine wrote something on the piece of paper, rolled it up and said, "Please give this to your little girl." Then he said goodbye, putting a hand on each shoulder and looking him in the eye.

The old man watched as he disappeared and knew he would never see him again. |
| *Place the scroll on the underlay beside the booklet. Put the crocus inside.* | That night when he went home he gave the rolled up piece of paper to his little girl. |
| *Unroll the scroll to reveal the "valentine" and allow the crocus to fall onto the underlay.* | She asked, "What does it say father?" Just then a crocus that had been rolled up in the paper fell to the floor. The old man read, "From your Valentine." |

COMPLETE LAYOUT OF THE STORY OF "ST." VALENTINE

MOVEMENTS	WORDS
	When the little girl picked up the flower to her great surprise she could see it.
	We remember Valentine because he loved so well.
Guide the wondering about Valentine's life by using these wondering questions.	I wonder what parts of Valentine's story you like the best?
	I wonder what part of the story is the most important?
	I wonder what part of the story is about you or where you might be in the story?
	I wonder if we could leave out any part of the story and still have all the story that we need?
Show the children the booklet. Point out the map of the world showing where Valentine lived, the flag of the country, the time line showing when he lived, and the story printed in the booklet to help the children know Valentine better.	Let me show you what is inside this booklet and how you can use it to find out more about Valentine.
Model how to put the lesson back on the tray and then carry it back to its spot on the shelf.	Now let me show you how to put the story away. Here is the mortar and pestle for making medicine; here is the crocus like the ones the little girl liked to pick; and here is the letter like the one Valentine wrote to the little girl. Here is the booklet that helps us remember Valentine. Here is the green (or purple) underlay, because we remember Valentine during the green and growing time of the year.
Return to your spot on the circle and begin to dismiss the children to their work.	Now I wonder what you would like to make your work today?

LESSON 5

THE STORY OF ST. PATRICK
(REMEMBERED MARCH 17, DIED IN 461)

LESSON NOTES

FOCUS: ST. PATRICK TRAVELED FOR GOD.

THE MATERIAL

- LOCATION: THE MYSTERY OF PENTECOST SHELF, SECOND SHELF, NEXT TO "ST." VALENTINE
- PIECES: ST. PATRICK BOOKLET, A BOAT, A SHEPHERD'S STAFF, A THREE-LEAF CLOVER
- UNDERLAY: PURPLE FELT

BACKGROUND

The place of Patrick's birth is unknown, but it was probably in the West of England or Scotland. He was born about the year 390. He was probably part Welsh and part Roman. For about thirty years he spread the Christian faith throughout Ireland and established many churches, monasteries and schools until he died when he was about 70.

NOTES ON THE MATERIAL

St. Patrick's story sits on a small, shallow tray about 8 inches square, with sides about two inches deep. It has a groove in the front to slide the "saint booklet" in so the children can see it when they approach the Mystery of Pentecost shelf.

The booklet is 4.25" x 5.5". The cover has an image of St. Patrick on it that matches the saint figure used in the introductory lessons on the communion of saints. The second page has a map of the world on it, with Ireland, Patrick's home, highlighted and labeled. It also has an image of the flag of Ireland on it. The third page has a time line beginning with the year 1 AD and ending with the year 2000 AD. It has an arrow indicating when Patrick lived. The rest of the booklet has the story of the life of Patrick.

Behind the booklet in the tray are placed the objects used to help us remember Patrick's life: A boat, a shepherd's staff and a three-leaf clover. The underlay is a 12" square piece of purple cloth and is folded on top of the objects.

ST. PATRICK TRAY

A NOTE ABOUT DATES FOR THE SAINTS

There is scholarly debate about the dates for the lives of many saints. We have had to make decisions about these dates for pedagogical reasons. We hope the children will continue to learn more about the saints all their life long, including their dates. The basis for the dates used in this volume is how they are remembered liturgically. This has been established by custom in the Roman Catholic, Anglican, and other traditions. We usually follow the dates that are found in the Episcopal publication called *Lesser Feasts and Fasts, 2006*. This book is also a reference for remembering saints for most days in the year and for children (and adults) to continue to learn more about the saints, using this liturgical orientation.

You can order this book at *www.morehouseducation.org* or by calling: 1-800-242-1918.

WHERE TO FIND MATERIALS

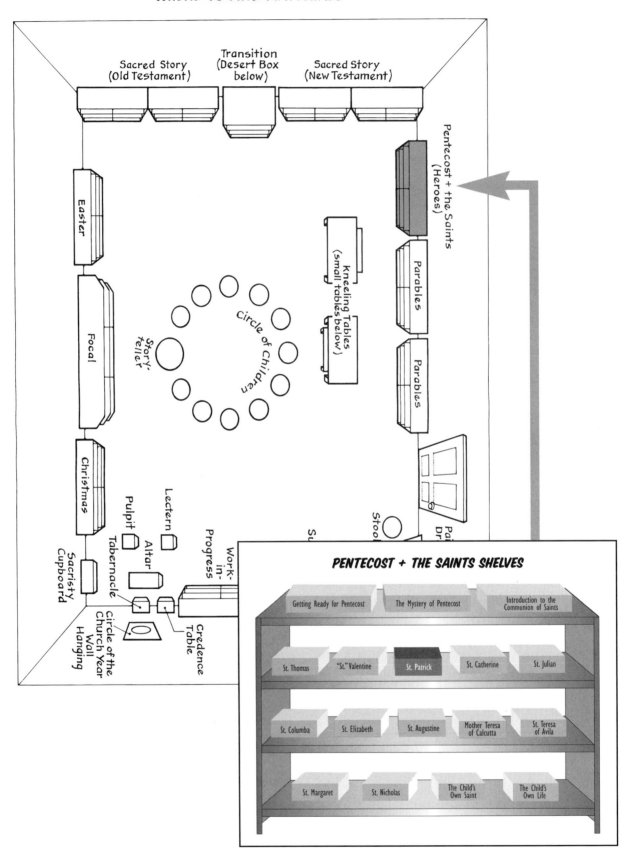

Sacred Story (Old Testament)

Transition (Desert Box below)

Sacred Story (New Testament)

Pentecost + the Saints (Heroes)

Easter

Focal

Christmas

Story-teller

Circle of Children

Kneeling Tables (small tables below)

Parables

Parables

Lectern

Pulpit

Altar

Tabernacle

Work-in-Progress

Credence Table

circle of the Church Year Wall Hanging

Sacristy Cupboard

Stool

PENTECOST + THE SAINTS SHELVES

Getting Ready for Pentecost	The Mystery of Pentecost	Introduction to the Communion of Saints
St. Thomas	"St." Valentine	St. Patrick	St. Catherine	St. Julian
St. Columba	St. Elizabeth	St. Augustine	Mother Teresa of Calcutta	St. Teresa of Avila
St. Margaret	St. Nicholas	The Child's Own Saint	The Child's Own Life

MOVEMENTS	WORDS
Go and get the material for St. Patrick's story.	Watch where I go to get the lesson for today.
Unfold the underlay in front of you and say:	This is the story of St. Patrick. The church remembers him during the season of Lent, a time of the color purple. I wonder *why* we remember Patrick? Let's see.
Take the saint booklet from the tray and place it in the center of the underlay.	Patrick was probably born in the northwest of England. When he was a little boy, he heard the sound that nobody wanted to hear. It was the crunching and scraping of the Irish boats as they were pulled up on the beach. They had come to steal children.
Put the boat on the underlay beside the booklet.	They took Patrick across the Irish sea. When they got to the other side they sold him. The man who bought Patrick made him a shepherd. He sent him into the wild country to take care of the sheep by himself with a few dogs to help.
Put the shepherd's staff on the underlay beside the booklet.	Patrick took good care of the sheep. He was a good shepherd, and the dogs understood and loved him. They worked together. Patrick prayed 100 times a day for all of them. One day Patrick told the dogs to take care of the sheep and left. He had to travel at night so no one could catch him. After many nights he began to smell salt in the air. As day was beginning to dawn, he heard the waves crashing on the shore. Patrick crept to the edge of a cliff and looked over. Down below was a ship that was about to sail for England, but the sailors couldn't get the big Irish dogs into the boat. They wanted to sell them in England, but the dogs did not want to go. They had black and brown, wiry hair, and were very tall and fierce.
Touch the boat.	Patrick climbed down the cliff and walked into the midst of the dogs. He sat down and began to talk to them. When Patrick went on the boat the dogs followed him, so the sailors decided Patrick could go with them. When he got home he decided he wanted to go back to school so he could be a priest. The children thought it was strange because he was so much older and taller than any of them. He didn't care because he wanted to learn to read.

MOVEMENTS	WORDS
	Patrick became a priest. One night he dreamed that God wanted him to go back to Ireland. "Come back we are waiting for you," the people said in the dream.
	He went.
Touch the shepherd's staff.	Patrick was the first Bishop for Ireland, another kind of shepherd. It took a lot of courage to go there. The people in Ireland did not like Christian people. Some tried to hurt him and even kill him. Patrick didn't care. He loved being a priest and loved telling people that God is love.
	He taught like this:
Put the three-leaf clover on the underlay.	One day someone asked him what the Holy Trinity was. How could there be three Gods and yet only one God? Patrick smiled, and with a twinkle in his eye leaned over and picked a shamrock. He said, "See, three leaves in one and one in three."
	When he was an old man he continued to worry about Ireland. He climbed a great hill and prayed for Ireland and its future. And if you go there today you can still climb that very hill to pray.
	We remember Patrick, because he traveled for God.

COMPLETE LAYOUT OF THE STORY OF ST. PATRICK

MOVEMENTS

Guide the wondering about Patrick's life by using these wondering questions.

Show the children the booklet. Point out the map of the world showing where Patrick lived, the flag of the country, the time line showing when he lived, and the story printed to help the children know Patrick better.

Model how to put the lesson back on the and then carry it back to its spot on the shelf.

Return to your spot on the circle and begin to dismiss the children to their work.

WORDS

I wonder what parts of Patrick's story you like the best?

I wonder what part of the story is the most important?

I wonder what part of the story is about you or where you might be in the story?

I wonder if we could leave out any part of the story and still have all the story that we need?

Let me show you what is inside this booklet and how you can use it to find out more about Patrick.

Now let me show you how to put the story away. Here is the boat like the one Patrick traveled on. Here is the shepherd's staff that reminds us that Patrick was a good shepherd to the sheep when he was a boy, and a different sort of shepherd when he became the Bishop of Ireland. Here is the three-leaf clover, also called a *shamrock*, that Patrick used to teach the people about the Holy Trinity. Here is the booklet that helps us remember Patrick. And here is the purple underlay, because we remember Patrick during the season of Lent, a time of the color purple.

Now I wonder what you would like to make your work today?

LESSON 6

THE STORY OF ST. CATHERINE OF SIENA (REMEMBERED APRIL 29, DIED IN 1380)

LESSON NOTES

FOCUS: ST. CATHERINE OF SIENA SHOWED PEOPLE HOW TO BE FAIR FOR GOD.

THE MATERIAL

- **LOCATION: THE MYSTERY OF PENTECOST SHELF, SECOND SHELF, NEXT TO ST. PATRICK**
- **PIECES: ST. CATHERINE OF SIENA BOOKLET, A LILY, A LETTER, A BRIDGE**
- **UNDERLAY: WHITE**

BACKGROUND

Catherine was born in 1347 and became a nun at the age of 16. She was known for her visions and the strict life she led, but also because she negotiated peace between Italian cities and helped persuade the Pope to return to Rome from France. She died in 1380 when she was only about 33 years old. She was declared one of the 33 Doctors of the Church in 1970, one of only three women.

NOTES ON THE MATERIAL

St. Catherine of Siena's story sits on a small, shallow tray about 8 inches square, with sides about two inches deep. It has a groove in the front to slide the "saint booklet" in so the children can see it when they approach the Mystery of Pentecost shelf.

The booklet is 4.25" x 5.5". The cover has an image of St. Catherine of Siena on it that matches the saint figure used in the introductory lessons on the communion of saints. The second page has a map of the world on it, with Italy, Catherine's home, highlighted and labeled. It also has an image of the flag of Italy. The third page has a time line beginning with the year 1 AD and ending with the year 2000 AD. It has an arrow indicating when Catherine lived. The rest of the booklet has the story of the life of Catherine.

Behind the booklet in the tray are placed the objects used to help us remember Catherine's life: A lily, a letter and a stone bridge. The underlay is a 12" square piece of white cloth and is folded on top of the objects.

ST. CATHERINE OF SIENA TRAY

A NOTE ABOUT DATES FOR THE SAINTS

There is scholarly debate about the dates for the lives of many saints. We have had to make decisions about these dates for pedagogical reasons. We hope the children will continue to learn more about the saints all their life long, including their dates. The basis for the dates used in this volume is how they are remembered liturgically. This has been established by custom in the Roman Catholic, Anglican, and other traditions. We usually follow the dates that are found in the Episcopal publication called *Lesser Feasts and Fasts, 2006*. This book is also a reference for remembering saints for most days in the year and for children (and adults) to continue to learn more about the saints, using this liturgical orientation.

You can order this book at *www.morehouseeducation.org* or by calling: 1-800-242-1918.

WHERE TO FIND MATERIALS

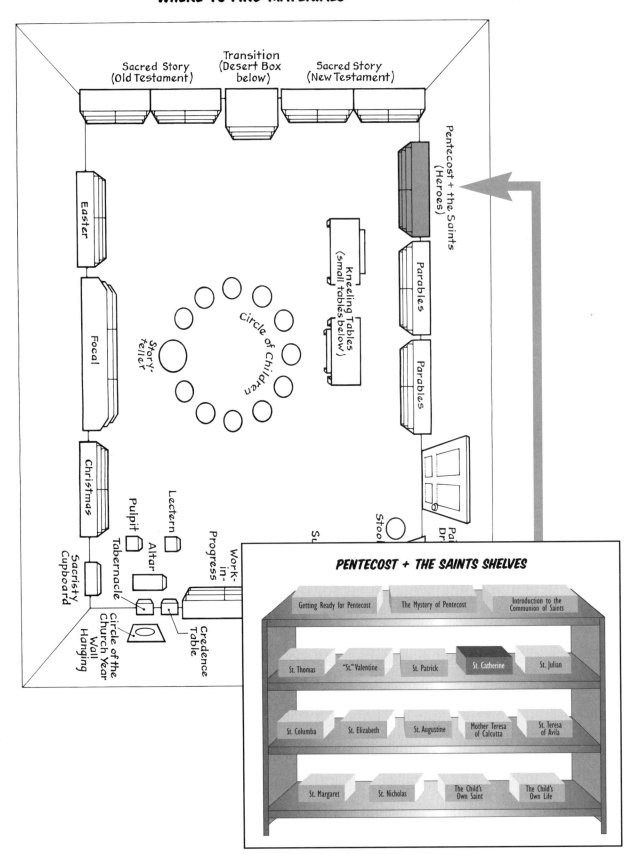

Sacred Story (Old Testament)

Transition (Desert Box below)

Sacred Story (New Testament)

Pentecost + the Saints (Heroes)

Easter

Focal

Christmas

Story-teller

circle of Children

Kneeling Tables (small tables below)

Parables

Parables

Lectern

Pulpit

Altar

Tabernacle

Work-in-Progress

Stool

Credence Table

circle of the Church Year Wall Hanging

Sacristy Cupboard

PENTECOST + THE SAINTS SHELVES

Getting Ready for Pentecost | The Mystery of Pentecost | Introduction to the Communion of Saints

St. Thomas | "St." Valentine | St. Patrick | St. Catherine | St. Julian

St. Columba | St. Elizabeth | St. Augustine | Mother Teresa of Calcutta | St. Teresa of Avila

St. Margaret | St. Nicholas | The Child's Own Saint | The Child's Own Life

MOVEMENTS	WORDS
Go and get the material for St. Catherine of Siena's story.	Watch where I go to get the lesson for today.
Unfold the underlay in front of you and say:	This is the story of St. Catherine of Siena. The church remembers Catherine during the season of Easter, a time of the color white. I wonder *why* we remember Catherine? Let's see.
Take the saint booklet from the tray and place it in the center of the underlay.	Catherine was born in a city of steep streets and red tiled roofs. The name of the city was Siena. It is in Italy. She was the 24th of 25 children. Her house was very crowded. She still found plenty of time to be with God, so that when she was only 7 she knew that what she wanted to do was to come even closer.

Catherine also began to look for ways to help people, so she served as a nurse in homes and hospitals. People were amazed at the many things she could do. Catherine grew especially busy helping people when the black plague came, when so many were sick and died.

One time she went to Florence, another city in Italy, and met Raymond of Capua (Kap-ya) who helped her on her spiritual journey. When she was older she said in one of her letters that he was like both a father and a son given to her by the mother Mary. |
| *Place the letter on the underlay beside the booklet.* | One time she wrote to Raymond of Capua, "Pardon me for writing too much, but my hands and tongue go along with my heart." She liked to write letters. |
| *Place the lily on the underlay.* | Catherine had a passion for flowers and liked to weave them into little crosses for her close friends. She often dreamed that angels descended from heaven and crowned her with white lilies.

People noticed how holy she was so they asked her to travel to other cities to help them discover what was fair when they fought against each other. She loved the little group of friends she traveled with. They were like a flock of birds.

Even the church was fighting. It had different leaders called popes. One of the popes moved to France during the fighting. She tried to help him make peace with the city of Florence and failed, but she did convince the pope to go back to Rome to live. |

MOVEMENTS

Place the bridge on the underlay.

Note: If asked who the other two were, you can tell the children St. Teresa of Avila (d. 1582) and St. Therese of Lisieux (d. 1897).

WORDS

One of the most important things Catherine wrote was a book called *The Dialogue*. It was a conversation she had with her soul. In that famous book she wrote how Jesus was like a bridge. The bridge had stone walls and a roof so the travelers would not fall off or get wet when it rains. It makes it possible to go from where you are now to where God is.

Finally Catherine wore out. She was still young, but could no longer eat or even swallow water. She went to St. Peter's Church in Rome each morning for Mass and spent the day in prayer. Finally she couldn't walk. She died in the spring when she was only thirty-three years old.

The Roman Catholic church in all its history has honored only three women with the title of Doctor of the Church. Catherine of Siena was one of these.

We remember Catherine for many reasons, but most of all because she showed people how to be fair for God.

COMPLETE LAYOUT OF THE STORY OF ST. CATHERINE OF SIENA

MOVEMENTS

Guide the wondering about Catherine's life by using these wondering questions.

Show the children the booklet. Point out the map of the world showing where Catherine lived, the flag of the country, the time line showing when she lived, and the story printed to help the children know Catherine better.

Model how to put the lesson back on the tray and then carry it back to its spot on the shelf.

Return to your spot on the circle and begin to dismiss the children to their work.

WORDS

I wonder what parts of Catherine's story you like the best?

I wonder what part of the story is the most important?

I wonder what part of the story is about you or where you might be in the story?

I wonder if we could leave any part of the story out and still have all the story that we need?

Let me show you what is inside this booklet and how you can use it to find out more about Catherine.

Now let me show you how to put the story away. Here is letter like one Catherine wrote. Here is the lily that reminds us of Catherine's love for flowers and her dream about the angels coming from heaven to crown her with lilies. Here is the bridge that reminds us how Catherine taught that Jesus was like a bridge. Here is the booklet that helps us remember Catherine. And here is the white underlay, because we remember Catherine during the season of Easter.

Now I wonder what you would like to make your work today?

LESSON 7

ST. JULIAN OF NORWICH
(REMEMBERED MAY 8, DIED ABOUT 1417)

LESSON NOTES

FOCUS: ST. JULIAN OF NORWICH WAS QUIET AND WISE FOR GOD.

THE MATERIAL

- LOCATION: THE MYSTERY OF PENTECOST SHELF, SECOND SHELF, NEXT TO ST. CATHERINE OF SIENA
- PIECES: ST. JULIAN OF NORWICH BOOKLET, A LITTLE STONE BUILDING WITH A WINDOW IN IT, A HAZELNUT, A PLAQUE WITH THE WORDS, "ALL SHALL BE WELL, AND ALL SHALL BE WELL, AND ALL MANNER OF THING SHALL BE WELL."
- UNDERLAY: WHITE

BACKGROUND

Julian was born in 1342 and is associated with Norwich, England. On May 8, 1373 when she was thirty she received a series of revelations and then become an anchorite, living alone in a cell attached to St. Julian's Church in Norwich. She almost certainly took the name by which we know her from that church. Her book, *Showings*, was the first book to be written by a woman in English.

NOTES ON THE MATERIAL

St. Julian of Norwich's story sits on a small, shallow tray about 8 inches square, with sides about two inches deep. It has a groove in the front to slide the "saint booklet" in so the children can see it when they approach the Mystery of Pentecost shelf.

The booklet is 4.25" x 5.5". The cover has an image of St. Julian of Norwich on it that matches the saint figure used in the introductory lessons on the communion of saints. The second page has a map of the world on it, with England, Julian's home, highlighted and labeled. It also has an image of the flag of the United Kingdom since England is part of the United Kingdom. The third page has a time line beginning with the year 1 AD and ending with the year 2000 AD. It has an arrow indicating when Julian lived. The rest of the booklet has the story of the life of Julian.

Behind the booklet in the tray are placed the objects used to help us remember Julian's life: A little stone building with a window in it, a hazelnut and a plaque with the words, "All shall be well, and all shall be well, and all manner of thing shall be well." The underlay is a 12" square piece of white cloth and is folded on top of the objects.

ST. JULIAN OF NORWICH TRAY

A NOTE ABOUT DATES FOR THE SAINTS

There is scholarly debate about the dates for the lives of many saints. We have had to make decisions about these dates for pedagogical reasons. We hope the children will continue to learn more about the saints all their life long, including their dates. The basis for the dates used in this volume is how they are remembered liturgically. This has been established by custom in the Roman Catholic, Anglican, and other traditions. We usually follow the dates that are found in the Episcopal publication called *Lesser Feasts and Fasts, 2006*. This book is also a reference for remembering saints for most days in the year and for children (and adults) to continue to learn more about the saints, using this liturgical orientation.

You can order this book at *www.morehouseeducation.org* or by calling: 1-800-242-1918.

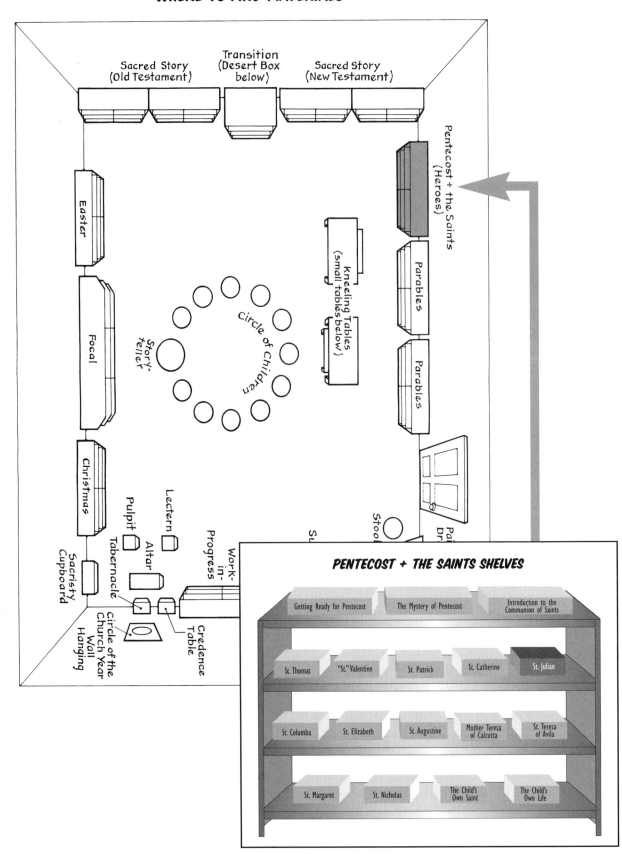

PENTECOST + THE SAINTS SHELVES

MOVEMENTS	WORDS
Go and get the material for St. Julian of Norwich's story.	Watch where I go to get the lesson for today.
Unfold the underlay in front of you and say:	This is the story of St. Julian of Norwich. The church remembers her during the season of Easter, a time of the color white. I wonder *why* we remember Julian? Let's see.
Take the saint booklet from the tray and place it in the center of the underlay.	Not very much is known about Julian. We don't know where she was born or what her family was like. But we do know that she was quiet, and her way of coming close to God was to be by herself.
Place the little stone building on the underlay beside the booklet.	She had a little stone building made in which she lived all alone, by the church of St. Julian in Norwich, which is in England. The church still stands to this day. Her little room was destroyed by bombs during the Second World War, but it has been rebuilt just like it was.
	Julian was not always alone. Many say she enjoyed the company of a cat, and people came to talk to her because they heard that she was very wise and holy.
	She wrote down some things about God in a book called *Showings*. It was the first book to be written in English by a woman.
Place the hazelnut on the underlay.	She wrote how one time God came to her and showed her something no bigger than a hazelnut lying in the palm of her hand. She wondered what it could be. God said, "It is everything that I have made." She wrote, "I was amazed, because it was so little. Why didn't it fall into nothing?" (Chapter 4, short text) God said, "It lasts and always will because God loves it." So everything lasts because of God's love.
	Sometimes when Julian was thinking and writing about God she called God her mother. She was not the first to do this, but she did so with great care. She wanted to unite the motherhood of God and the fatherhood of God because God is bigger than either word about God. She said that in the Holy Trinity, "Fatherhood means power and goodness while motherhood means wisdom and lovingness."

MOVEMENTS

WORDS

Put the plaque down with these words.

She had many questions about God, but the answer to all of them was that whatever God does is done in love, and that "…all shall be well, and all shall be well, and all manner (of) things shall be well" (13th Revelation, Chapter 27).

Julian remained in her cell until she died. We remember Julian because she was quiet and wise for God.

COMPLETE LAYOUT OF THE STORY OF ST. JULIAN OF NORWICH

Guide the wondering about Julian's life using these wondering questions.

I wonder what parts of Julian's story you like the best?

I wonder what part of the story is the most important?

I wonder what part of the story is about you or where you might be in the story?

I wonder if we could leave any part of the story out and still have all the story that we need?

Show the children the booklet. Point out the map of the world showing where Julian lived, the flag of the country, the time line showing when she lived, and the story printed to help the children know Julian better.

Let me show you what is inside this booklet and how you might work with it yourself.

MOVEMENTS

Model how to put the lesson back on the tray and then carry it back to its spot on the shelf.

Return to your spot on the circle and begin to dismiss the children to their work.

WORDS

Now let me show you how to put the story away. Here is the little stone house like the one Julian lived in. Here is the book she wrote about her visions of God. Here is the hazelnut that reminds us of the time God told her of his love for creation. Here are the words God gave Julian to comfort her, "…All shall be well, and all shall be well, and all manner (of) thing shall be well." Here is the booklet that helps us remember all about Julian. And here is the white underlay, because we remember Julian during the season of Easter, a time of the color white.

Now I wonder what you would like to make your work today?

LESSON 8

THE STORY OF ST. COLUMBA
(REMEMBERED JUNE 9, DIED IN 597)

LESSON NOTES

FOCUS: ST. COLUMBA LOVED BOOKS AND PEOPLE FOR GOD.

THE MATERIAL

● LOCATION: THE MYSTERY OF PENTECOST SHELF, THIRD SHELF, UNDER ST. THOMAS

● PIECES: ST. COLUMBA BOOKLET, A DOVE, AN ILLUMINATED MANUSCRIPT PAGE, A PHOTO OF IONA

● UNDERLAY: GREEN

BACKGROUND

Columba was born in Donegal, Ireland in 521 where one of his ancestors was the high king. He became a monk and then a priest and founded many monasteries and churches in Ireland. He moved to the Island of Iona in 563 which provided a place for prayer, the copying of books, and a base to help establish Christianity in the British Isles.

NOTES ON THE MATERIAL

St. Columba's story sits on a small, shallow tray about 8 inches square, with sides about two inches deep. It has a groove in the front to slide the "saint booklet" in so the children can see it when they approach the Mystery of Pentecost shelf.

The booklet is 4.25" x 5.5". The cover has an image of St. Columba on it that matches the saint figure used in the introductory lessons on the communion of saints. The second page has a map of the world on it, with Scotland, Columba's home, high-lighted and labeled. It also has an image of the flag of the United Kingdom since Scot-land is part of that country. The third page has a time line beginning with the year 1 AD and ending with the year 2000 AD. It has an arrow indicating when Columba lived. The rest of the booklet has the story of the life of Columba.

Behind the booklet in the tray are placed the objects used to help us remember Columba's life: A dove, an illuminated manuscript page mounted on wood and a photo of Iona (laminated or mounted on wood). The underlay is a 12" square piece of green cloth and is folded on top of the objects.

ST. COLUMBA TRAY

A NOTE ABOUT DATES FOR THE SAINTS

There is scholarly debate about the dates for the lives of many saints. We have had to make decisions about these dates for pedagogical reasons. We hope the children will continue to learn more about the saints all their life long, including their dates. The basis for the dates used in this volume is how they are remembered liturgically. This has been established by custom in the Roman Catholic, Anglican, and other traditions. We usually follow the dates that are found in the Episcopal publication called *Lesser Feasts and Fasts, 2006*. This book is also a reference for remembering saints for most days in the year and for children (and adults) to continue to learn more about the saints, using this liturgical orientation.

You can order this book at *www.morehouseeducation.org* or by calling: 1-800-242-1918.

WHERE TO FIND MATERIALS

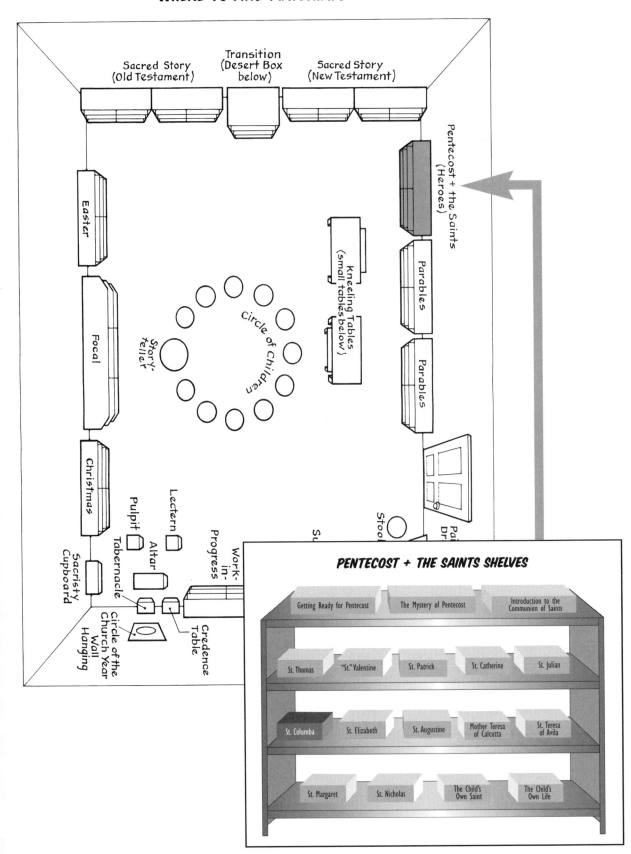

PENTECOST + THE SAINTS SHELVES

MOVEMENTS	WORDS
Go and get the material for St. Columba's story.	Watch where I go to get the lesson for today.
Unfold the underlay in front of you and say:	This is the story of St. Columba. The church remembers him during the green and growing time of the church year—after Pentecost. I wonder *why* we remember Columba? Let's see.
Take the saint booklet from the tray and place it in the center of the underlay.	
Place the dove beside the booklet on the underlay.	The name Columba means *the dove*. People sometimes said of Columba, "He had the face of an angel." They also said he was loving to all, but he was not always like that.
Put the page of illuminated manuscript on the underlay beside the booklet.	When Columba was a young man he was a monk. He loved books. He and the other monks made hundreds of copies of books with beautiful handwriting and tiny pictures.
	One day he made a copy of a book just for himself. It was Finnian's book. Finnian found out about Columba's secret copy and grew angry. The dispute was taken to the high king of Ireland, who decided against Columba. He said "to every cow her calf, to every book its copy." Columba had to give his copy to Finnian. Now Columba was angry and he started a war against the high king. Many people were killed.
	Columba was sorry. He loved books, but he also loved people. How could so many people be killed about a book? He decided to leave Ireland and try to tell about God's forgiveness to as many people as he could; to help people understand the danger of anger.
	Columba went to Scotland. He and twelve friends went in tiny boats to a small island off the coast to make their home. Their home was only three miles long and two miles wide. King Brude of Scotland gave them the island, because he could see that Columba was a good person. The name of the island was Iona. You can still visit there today.

MOVEMENTS

Put down the picture of Iona.

WORDS

On the island the monks built a tiny church and lived in small huts around it. They farmed the land and fished in the sea. They raised animals to give them clothing and food.

COMPLETE LAYOUT OF THE STORY OF ST. COLUMBA

The monks also made beautiful books and traveled all over Scotland to tell people, even kings, about God and the danger of anger. They also set up more communities like theirs on other islands.

The people of Scotland loved Columba so much that when King Conall died they let Columba choose the new King. He chose King Aiden, a Christian, who was a good King.

Columba lived on the Island of Iona for 34 years. By the time he died many people came to visit the island to pray and invited the monks to come and pray with them.

One day when he was very old Columba was copying the Bible and came to Psalm 34, verse 10, "...those who seek the Lord lack no good thing." He said, "Here at the end of this page I must stop." The next day he died, but many, many people had discovered the danger of anger and had become Christian because of him. He was happy.

We remember Columba because he loved books and people for God.

MOVEMENTS

Guide the wondering about Columba's life using these wondering questions.

Show the children the booklet. Point out the map of the world showing where Columba lived, the flag of the country, the time line showing when he lived, and the story printed to help the children know Columba better.

Model how to put the lesson back on the tray and then carry it back to its spot on the shelf.

Return to your spot on the circle and begin to dismiss the children to their work.

WORDS

I wonder what parts of Columba's story you like the best?

I wonder what part of the story is the most important?

I wonder what part of the story is about you or where you might be in the story?

I wonder if we could leave any part of the story out and still have all the story that we need?

Let me show you what is inside this booklet and how you might work with it yourself.

Now let me show you how to put the story away. Here is the dove from which Columba got his name. But we know he wasn't always peaceful like the dove. Here is the page from a book, like the one Columba loved and copied. Here is a picture of the island Columba lived on. Here is the booklet that helps us remember Columba. And here is the green underlay, because we remember Columba during the green and growing time of the year—the Sundays after Pentecost.

Now I wonder what you would like to make your work today?

LESSON 9

THE STORY OF ST. ELIZABETH OF PORTUGAL (REMEMBERED JULY 4, DIED IN 1336)

LESSON NOTES

FOCUS: ST. ELIZABETH OF PORTUGAL WAS PEACEFUL AND MADE PEACE FOR GOD.

THE MATERIAL

● LOCATION: THE MYSTERY OF PENTECOST SHELF, THIRD SHELF, BESIDE ST. COLUMBA

● PIECES: ST ELIZABETH OF PORTUGAL BOOKLET, PINE TREE, RED ROSES, DONKEY

● UNDERLAY: GREEN FELT

BACKGROUND

Elizabeth was born sometime around 1271 in what is now Spain and was named for her Great Aunt, St. Elizabeth of Hungary (1207-1231). When she was about 12 she was married to Dennis the King of Portugal. She was renowned for her service to the poor and her many good works, which helped create what many call the golden age of Portugal.

NOTES ON THE MATERIAL

St. Elizabeth's story sits on a small, shallow tray about 8 inches square, with sides about two inches deep. It has a groove in the front to slide the "saint booklet" in so the children can see it when they approach the Mystery of Pentecost shelf.

The booklet is 4.25" x 5.5". The cover has an image of St. Elizabeth on it that matches the saint figure used in the introductory lessons on the communion of saints. The second page has a map of the world on it, with Portugal, Elizabeth's home, highlighted and labeled. It also has an image of the flag of Portugal. The third page has a time line beginning with the year 1 AD and ending with the year 2000 AD. It has an arrow indicating when Elizabeth lived. The rest of the booklet has the story of the life of Elizabeth.

Behind the booklet in the tray are placed the objects used to help us remember Elizabeth's life: a pine tree, a small bunch of roses and a donkey. The underlay is a 12" square piece of green cloth and is folded on top of the objects.

ST. ELIZABETH OF PORTUGAL TRAY

A NOTE ABOUT DATES FOR THE SAINTS

There is scholarly debate about the dates for the lives of many saints. We have had to make decisions about these dates for pedagogical reasons. We hope the children will continue to learn more about the saints all their life long, including their dates. The basis for the dates used in this volume is how they are remembered liturgically. This has been established by custom in the Roman Catholic, Anglican, and other traditions. We usually follow the dates that are found in the Episcopal publication called *Lesser Feasts and Fasts, 2006*. This book is also a reference for remembering saints for most days in the year and for children (and adults) to continue to learn more about the saints, using this liturgical orientation.

You can order this book at *www.morehouseeducation.org*
or by calling: 1-800-242-1918.

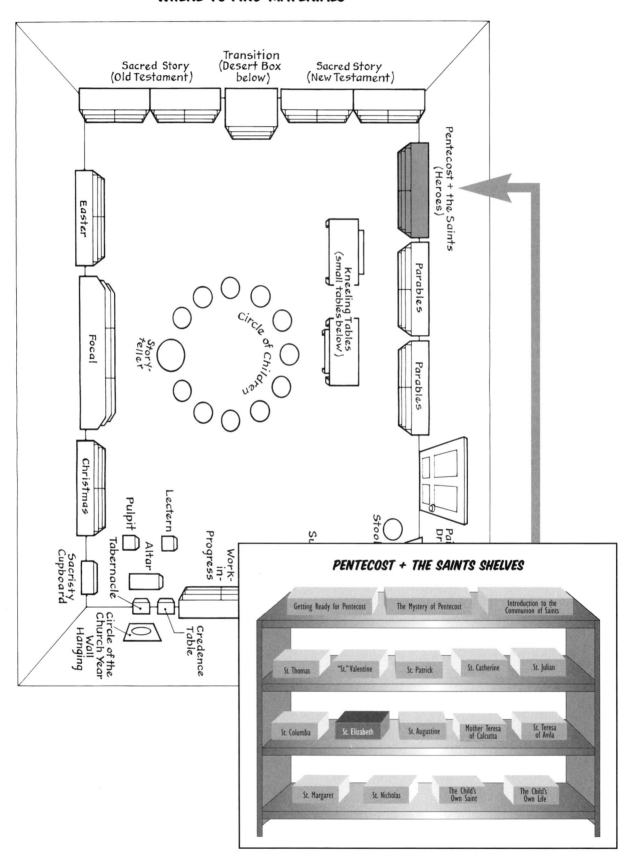

Sacred Story (Old Testament)

Transition (Desert Box below)

Sacred Story (New Testament)

Pentecost + the Saints (Heroes)

Easter

Focal

Christmas

Story-teller

Circle of Children

Kneeling Tables (small tables below)

Parables

Parables

Stool

Sacristy Cupboard

Tabernacle

Altar

Pulpit

Lectern

Work-in-Progress

Circle of the Church Year Wall Hanging

Credence Table

PENTECOST + THE SAINTS SHELVES

Getting Ready for Pentecost

The Mystery of Pentecost

Introduction to the Communion of Saints

St. Thomas

"St." Valentine

St. Patrick

St. Catherine

St. Julian

St. Columba

St. Elizabeth

St. Augustine

Mother Teresa of Calcutta

St. Teresa of Avila

St. Margaret

St. Nicholas

The Child's Own Saint

The Child's Own Life

MOVEMENTS	WORDS
Go and get the material for St. Elizabeth of Portugal's story.	Watch where I go to get the lesson for today.
Unfold the underlay in front of you and say:	This is the story of St. Elizabeth of Portugal. The church remembers her during the green and growing time of the church year—after Pentecost. I wonder *why* we remember Elizabeth? Let's see.
Take the saint booklet from the tray and place it in the center of the underlay.	When little Elizabeth was born she was named for her great Aunt, St. Elizabeth of Hungary. Elizabeth's family was always fighting, but not Elizabeth. Soon after she was born she went to live with her grandfather, who loved her very much.
	Her grandfather thought that she would become one of the greatest and most important women to come from his family, and he was right.
	When she was 6 she went back to live with her father, who ruled a part of Spain called Aragon. When she was 12 it was time for her to be married. Different kings wanted her for their sons, but her father gave her to Dennis of Portugal.
	Elizabeth had wanted to give herself to God alone, but she went to Portugal to be the wife of Dennis.
	When Elizabeth got to Portugal there were many parties and gifts, but she gave all her gifts to the poor.
	When she was 20 she gave birth to her first child, Constance. At 21 her son Alfonso was born.
	Elizabeth built a hospital for children who had been abandoned, shelters for poor travelers, hospitals for sick people, and a place for women to go where they would be forgiven for their troubles.
Place the pine tree on the underlay beside the booklet.	She also planted pine trees on the long beaches of her country to keep the sand from blowing or washing away. Elizabeth brought the seeds for the pine trees to the King in her apron.
	One time her husband was angry because she was giving so much money to the poor. He stopped her and said, "Let me see the money." When she showed him what she was carrying it was nothing but roses, but the roses later became gold.

MOVEMENTS	WORDS
Put the red roses on the underlay beside the booklet.	When Elizabeth's son grew up he went to war against his father. They faced each other across the battlefield. The arrows and rocks were flying. The two armies ran towards each other with a shout, and suddenly stopped. It grew quiet.
Put the donkey on the underlay.	There was Queen Elizabeth, riding on a mule, in-between the armies. She was so peaceful that the armies made peace.

The King died a year later in her arms. Now she could do what she always wanted to do. She went to live in a convent.

When she was old and dying Elizabeth called her daughter-in-law to bring a chair for the lady who had come to visit her. "What lady?" She asked, "The lady who is coming close now. The lady in white. You see, she is smiling." Elizabeth began to smile. It was as if she could see Mary, the mother of God, and Elizabeth began to pray. Then she died.

We remember Elizabeth because she was peaceful and made peace for God.

COMPLETE LAYOUT OF THE STORY OF ST. ELIZABETH OF PORTUGAL

MOVEMENTS	WORDS
Guide the wondering about Elizabeth's life using these wondering questions.	I wonder what parts of Elizabeth's story you like the best?
	I wonder what part of the story is the most important?
	I wonder what part of the story is about you or where you might be in the story?
	I wonder if we could leave any part of the story out and still have all the story that we need?
Show the children the booklet. Point out the map of the world showing where Elizabeth lived, the flag of the country, the time line showing when she lived, and the story printed to help the children know Elizabeth better.	Let me show you what is inside this booklet and how you might work with it yourself.
Model how to put the lesson back on the tray and then carry it back to its spot on the shelf.	Now let me show you how to put the story away. Here is the pine tree that reminds us that Elizabeth helped to save the beaches in Portugal by having pine trees planted. Here are the roses that remind us of the time King Dennis scolded Elizabeth for spending too much money. Here is the donkey that reminds of the time when Elizabeth rode into the battle between her husband and her son to make peace. Here is the booklet that helps us remember Elizabeth. And here is the green underlay, because we remember Elizabeth during the green and growing season of the year.
Return to your spot on the circle and begin to dismiss the children to their work.	Now I wonder what you would like to make your work today?

THE STORY OF ST. AUGUSTINE OF HIPPO (REMEMBERED AUG. 28, DIED IN 430)

LESSON NOTES

FOCUS: ST. AUGUSTINE OF HIPPO WAS RESTLESS AND FOUND REST IN GOD.

THE MATERIAL

- LOCATION: THE MYSTERY OF PENTECOST SHELF, THIRD SHELF, BESIDE ST. ELIZABETH
- PIECES: ST. AUGUSTINE OF HIPPO BOOKLET, A PEAR, THREE SMALL FELT CIRCLES (WHITE), CLOTH WITH A TEAR IN IT
- UNDERLAY: GREEN

BACKGROUND

Augustine was born in North Africa, lived for few years in Rome and Milan, and returned to Africa where he became a priest and bishop of Hippo. His many writings have influenced Christianity for more than 1500 years. He was the theologian most quoted by St. Thomas Aquinas.

NOTES ON THE MATERIAL

St. Augustine's story sits on a small, shallow tray about 8 inches square, with sides about two inches deep. It has a groove in the front to slide the "saint booklet" in so the children can see it when they approach the Mystery of Pentecost shelf.

The booklet is 4.25" x 5.5". The cover has an image of St. Augustine on it that matches the saint figure used in the introductory lessons on the communion of saints. The second page has a map of the world on it, with what we now call Algeria, Augustine's home, highlighted and labeled. It also has an image of the flag of Algeria. The third page has a time line beginning with the year 1 AD and ending with the year 2000 AD. It has an arrow indicating when Augustine lived. The rest of the booklet has the story of the life of Augustine.

Behind the booklet in the tray are placed the objects used to help us remember Augustine's life: a pear, three small felt circles (white) and a piece of cloth with a tear in it. The underlay is a 12" square piece of green cloth and is folded on top of the objects.

ST. AUGUSTINE OF HIPPO TRAY

A NOTE ABOUT DATES FOR THE SAINTS

There is scholarly debate about the dates for the lives of many saints. We have had to make decisions about these dates for pedagogical reasons. We hope the children will continue to learn more about the saints all their life long, including their dates. The basis for the dates used in this volume is how they are remembered liturgically. This has been established by custom in the Roman Catholic, Anglican, and other traditions. We usually follow the dates that are found in the Episcopal publication called *Lesser Feasts and Fasts, 2006*. This book is also a reference for remembering saints for most days in the year and for children (and adults) to continue to learn more about the saints, using this liturgical orientation.

You can order this book at *www.morehouseeducation.org* or by calling: 1-800-242-1918.

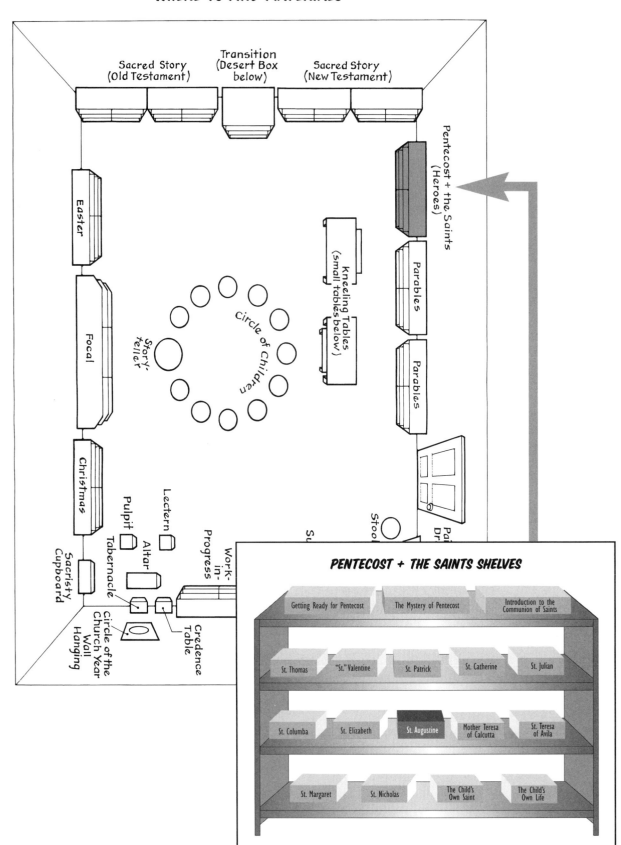

Sacred Story (Old Testament)

Transition (Desert Box below)

Sacred Story (New Testament)

Pentecost + the Saints (Heroes)

Easter

Focal

Christmas

Story-teller

circle of Children

kneeling Tables (small tables below)

Parables

Parables

Sacristy Cupboard

Pulpit

Lectern

Altar

Tabernacle

Work-in-Progress

circle of the Church Year Wall Hanging

Credence Table

Stool

PENTECOST + THE SAINTS SHELVES

| Getting Ready for Pentecost | The Mystery of Pentecost | Introduction to the Communion of Saints |

| St. Thomas | "St." Valentine | St. Patrick | St. Catherine | St. Julian |

| St. Columba | St. Elizabeth | St. Augustine | Mother Teresa of Calcutta | St. Teresa of Avila |

| St. Margaret | St. Nicholas | The Child's Own Saint | The Child's Own Life |

MOVEMENTS	WORDS
Go and get the material for St. Augustine of Hippo's story.	Watch where I go to get the lesson for today.
Unfold the underlay in front of you and say:	This is the story of St. Augustine of Hippo. The church remembers him during the green and growing time of the church year—after Pentecost. I wonder *why* we remember Augustine? Let's see.
Take the saint booklet from the tray and place it in the center of the underlay.	Augustine was born and lived most of his life in the part of North Africa we now call Algeria.
Put the pear on the underlay.	One day he stole pears from a tree. He wasn't hungry. He didn't sell them. He just took them and he couldn't figure out why. He would wonder all his life about why people did the things they were *not* supposed to, and didn't do the things they *were* supposed to.
	He didn't like school but he loved words. He was punished in school and the teachers made him feel ashamed, but he was very bright and did well anyway. He graduated from college in Carthage, one of the great cities along the northern coast of Africa, and then moved to Rome and then Milan, in what we now call Italy, to teach students how to make speeches.
	He went to "Italy" with his wife and son and his mother came later. He didn't want to be a Christian, but his mother never stopped praying for him to become one.
	The whole family moved from Rome to Milan. Ambrose, the Bishop of Milan, showed him that God *was* real, so Augustine and his son were baptized together and his mother was happy.
Put down the three white circles to mark this moment in his life—in the same way as you would for the baptism lesson, Vol. 3, *p. 70.*	He was baptized in the name of the Father and of the Son and the Holy Spirit and later wrote about the Holy Trinity. In his book about the Trinity he said God is love, but love is three in one: There is the one who loves, the one who is loved, and love itself. God made us like that too, so we can love God and each other well.
	Augustine soon returned to Africa where he became a priest and not long afterwards he was made the Bishop in a seaport city called Hippo. He was Bishop there for 35 years.

MOVEMENTS

Place the cloth with the tear in it on the underlay.

WORDS

He never stopped thinking about stealing those pears, and often felt restless so he wondered about evil. Where does it come from? God didn't make it because God is good. It didn't defeat God because God is all-powerful. God didn't forget or not know about it, because God knows everything. It is a defect, like a tear in a piece of cloth. Evil tears things down while God builds things up. God helps us do that too, so our restlessness can rest in God.

When he died his library, which was filled with his own books, was saved. No one knows how but everyone is happy because now we have his books to help us know more about God, too.

We remember Augustine because he was restless and found rest in God.

COMPLETE LAYOUT OF THE STORY OF ST. AUGUSTINE OF HIPPO

Guide the wondering about Augustine's life using these wondering questions.

I wonder what parts of Augustine's story you like the best?

I wonder what part of the story is the most important?

I wonder what part of the story is about you or where you might be in the story?

I wonder if we could leave any part of the story out and still have all the story that we need?

MOVEMENTS

Show the children the booklet. Point out the map of the world showing where Augustine lived, the flag of the country, the time line showing when he lived, and the story printed to help the children know Augustine better.

Model how to put the lesson back on the tray and then carry it back to its spot on the shelf.

Return to your spot on the circle and begin to dismiss the children to their work.

WORDS

Let me show you what is inside this booklet and how you might work with it yourself.

Now let me show you how to put the story away. Here is the pear that reminds us of how troubled Augustine was by evil in the world and in himself. Here are the three circles that mark the time when Augustine and his son were baptized and his book about the Trinity. Here is the cloth with a tear in it to reminds us of evil. Here is the booklet that helps us remember Augustine. Here is the green underlay, because we remember Augustine during the green and growing season of the year.

Now I wonder what you would like to make your work today?

THE STORY OF MOTHER TERESA OF CALCUTTA (DIED SEPT. 5, 1997)

LESSON NOTES

FOCUS: MOTHER TERESA OF CALCUTTA CARED FOR THE SICK AND POOR FOR GOD.

THE MATERIAL

- LOCATION: THE MYSTERY OF PENTECOST SHELF, THIRD SHELF, BESIDE ST. AUGUSTINE
- PIECES: MOTHER TERESA OF CALCUTTA BOOKLET, A SARI LIKE SHE WORE (WHITE WITH BLUE TRIM) WITH A CROSS PINNED TO IT, A BOWL & CLOTH, A WOODEN PLAQUE WITH THE IMAGE OF A DOVE AND THE WORD "PEACE."
- UNDERLAY: GREEN FELT

BACKGROUND

Agnes Gonxha Bojaxhiu was born of Albanian parents in Skopje in 1910 When she entered the Loreto convent in Ireland she took the name Teresa from Theresa of Lisieux at the age of 18. The nuns sent her to their convent in India where she took her final vows in 1937. In 1948 she left the convent to serve the poorest people in Calcutta. She won the Nobel Peace Prize in 1979. The nuns who continue her work are known as the Sisters of Charity. Teresa was beatified by the Roman Catholic Church in 2003, but has not yet been canonized, so she has no day of remembrance.

NOTES ON THE MATERIAL

Mother Teresa of Calcutta's story sits on a small, shallow tray about 8 inches square, with sides about two inches deep. It has a groove in the front to slide the booklet in so the children can see it when they approach the Mystery of Pentecost shelf.

The booklet is 4.25" x 5.5". The cover has an image of Teresa on it that matches the figure used in the introductory lessons on the communion of saints. The second page has a map of the world, with India, Teresa's home, highlighted and labeled. It also has an image of the flag of India. The third page has a time line beginning with the year 1 AD and ending with the year 2000 AD with an arrow indicating when Teresa lived. The rest of the booklet has the story of the life of Teresa.

Behind the booklet in the tray are placed the objects used to help us remember Teresa's life: a sari like she wore, a bowl and cloth and a wooden plaque with an image of a dove on it and the word *Peace*. The underlay is a 12" square piece of green cloth and is folded on top of the objects.

MOTHER TERESA OF CALCUTTA TRAY

A NOTE ABOUT DATES FOR THE SAINTS

There is scholarly debate about the dates for the lives of many saints. We have had to make decisions about these dates for pedagogical reasons. We hope the children will continue to learn more about the saints all their life long, including their dates. The basis for the dates used in this volume is how they are remembered liturgically. This has been established by custom in the Roman Catholic, Anglican, and other traditions. We usually follow the dates that are found in the Episcopal publication called *Lesser Feasts and Fasts, 2006*. This book is also a reference for remembering saints for most days in the year and for children (and adults) to continue to learn more about the saints, using this liturgical orientation.

You can order this book at *www.morehouseeducation.org* or by calling: 1-800-242-1918.

WHERE TO FIND MATERIALS

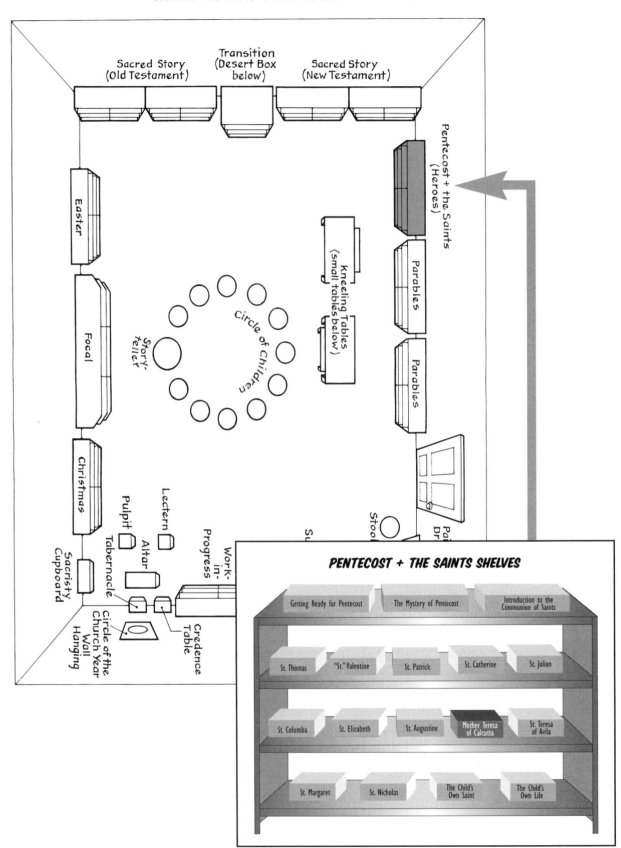

Sacred Story (Old Testament)

Transition (Desert Box below)

Sacred Story (New Testament)

Pentecost + the Saints (Heroes)

Easter

Focal

Christmas

Story-teller

Circle of Children

Kneeling Tables (small tables below)

Parables

Parables

Sacristy Cupboard

Pulpit

Lectern

Tabernacle

Altar

Work-in-Progress

Credence Table

Circle of the Church Year Wall Hanging

PENTECOST + THE SAINTS SHELVES

Getting Ready for Pentecost

The Mystery of Pentecost

Introduction to the Communion of Saints

St. Thomas

"St." Valentine

St. Patrick

St. Catherine

St. Julian

St. Columba

St. Elizabeth

St. Augustine

Mother Teresa of Calcutta

St. Teresa of Avila

St. Margaret

St. Nicholas

The Child's Own Saint

The Child's Own Life

MOVEMENTS	WORDS
Go and get the material for Mother Teresa of Calcutta's story.	Watch where I go to get the lesson for today.
Unfold the underlay in front of you and say:	This is the story of Mother Teresa of Calcutta. We shall remember her during the green and growing time of the church year—after Pentecost. I wonder *why* we remember Teresa? Let's see.
Take the saint booklet from the tray and place it in the center of the underlay.	A little girl named Agnes was born in Skopje (**SKAW**-pee-yeh), Macedonia to Albanian parents. Her father died when she was only eight years old, but her mother began her own business. She sewed beautiful things out of cloth.
	While Agnes was a teenager she became very close to God, so, in 1928, she left home to go to Ireland to the Loreto Convent in Dublin. When she joined the convent she was named Teresa.
	The nuns in Dublin then sent her to India where she became a Loreto nun in 1937. She lived mostly in Calcutta where she taught at St. Mary's, a school for wealthy girls.
	One day she found an old woman dying in the streets. She was so weak that the rats and ants had eaten part of her body. Teresa was not very big, but she picked up the lady and took her to a hospital. They would not let her in, so Teresa of Calcutta began to help all the people she could who had no place to go.
Place the sari, with a little cross pinned on it, on the underlay beside the booklet.	In 1948 she left the convent where she had been teaching and stopped wearing the black clothes of a nun. She chose instead to wear a sari like the ladies of India. It was white with a blue border on it and with a little cross fastened to her shoulder. Then she spent every day helping the poorest of the poor of Calcutta. She became a nurse to help more, especially the people who were dying alone on the street. She even wiped the flies out of their eyes.
Place the bowl and the cloth on the underlay beside the booklet.	In the 1950s she gathered her many helpers into a new religious order. They worked only with the poor as she did.
	Sister Teresa became known as Mother Teresa because she was like a mother to all her helpers. This new group was called the Missionaries of Charity. Charity is a kind of love that loves even if no one loves back.

MOVEMENTS

Place the wooden "Peace" plaque on the underlay.

WORDS

She helped the sick and dying but also worked for peace. One time she said, "If you want to work for peace don't talk to your friends, talk to your enemies." She did so much work for peace that she won the Nobel Peace Prize in 1979. When she went to receive the prize she gave the money of the prize and the food for the banquet to the poor.

She always knew what to do. When the Pope was shot in Rome she went immediately to see him. When there was a hospital full of children in danger in Beirut, she stopped the fighting until the children could be taken care of. When she had a heart attack in Rome, she went home to Calcutta. That was where she died.

Thousands of people came from all over the world to her funeral. She was carried through the streets to her burial in the same carriage that carried Gandhi, another great worker for peace, to his burial in India.

We remember Teresa, because she cared for the poor and sick for God.

COMPLETE LAYOUT OF THE STORY OF MOTHER TERESA OF CALCUTTA

MOVEMENTS

Guide the wondering about Teresa's life using these wondering questions.

Show the children the booklet. Point out the map of the world showing where Teresa lived, the flag of the country, the time line showing when she lived, and the story printed to help the children know Teresa better.

Model how to put the lesson back on the tray and then carry it back to its spot on the shelf.

Return to your spot in the circle and begin to dismiss the children to their work.

WORDS

I wonder what parts of Teresa's story you like the best?

I wonder what part of the story is the most important?

I wonder what part of the story is about you or where you might be in the story?

I wonder if we could leave any part of the story out and still have all the story that we need?

Let me show you what is inside this booklet and how you might work with it yourself.

Now let me show you how to put the story away. Here is the sari like the one Teresa wore after she started helping the poorest of the poor. Here is the bowl and the cloth that reminds us that Teresa learned how to be a nurse so she could care for the sick. Here is the plaque that reminds us how she worked for peace. Here is the booklet that helps us remember all about Teresa. And here is the green underlay, because we remember Teresa during the green and growing season of the year.

Now I wonder what you would like to make your work today?

THE STORY ST. TERESA OF AVILA
(REMEMBERED OCT. 15, DIED IN 1582)

LESSON NOTES

FOCUS: ST. TERESA OF AVILA WAS STRICT, BUT LAUGHED FOR GOD.

THE MATERIAL

- **LOCATION: THE MYSTERY OF PENTECOST SHELF, THIRD SHELF, BESIDE ST. TERESA OF CALCUTTA**
- **PIECES: ST. TERESA OF AVILA BOOKLET, A BED, A DONKEY, A CRYSTAL**
- **UNDERLAY: GREEN**

BACKGROUND

St. Teresa of Avila was born in what is now Spain as one of 10 children. When she was 14 she was sent to a convent school and was ill much of her early life. When she became a Carmelite nun she helped restore the strict rule of life to the nuns, but she led them with love and good humor. She is best known for her book *The Interior Castle*. Like Catherine of Siena the Roman Catholic Church declared her, in 1970, one of the three women Doctors of the Church—Theresa of Lisieux is the third

NOTES ON THE MATERIAL

St. Teresa of Avila's story sits on a small, shallow tray about 8 inches square, with sides about two inches deep. It has a groove in the front to slide the "saint booklet" in so the children can see it when they approach the Mystery of Pentecost shelf.

The booklet is 4.25" x 5.5". The cover has an image of St. Teresa on it that matches the saint figure used in the introductory lessons on the communion of saints. The second page has a map of the world on it, with Spain, Teresa's home, highlighted and labeled. It also has an image of the flag of Spain. The third page has a time line beginning with the year 1 AD and ending with the year 2000 AD. It has an arrow indicating when Teresa lived. The rest of the booklet has the story of the life of Teresa.

Behind the booklet in the tray are placed the objects used to help us remember Teresa's life: a cross, a donkey and a crystal. The underlay is a 12" square piece of green cloth and is folded on top of the objects.

ST. TERESA OF AVILA TRAY

A NOTE ABOUT DATES FOR THE SAINTS

There is scholarly debate about the dates for the lives of many saints. We have had to make decisions about these dates for pedagogical reasons. We hope the children will continue to learn more about the saints all their life long, including their dates. The basis for the dates used in this volume is how they are remembered liturgically. This has been established by custom in the Roman Catholic, Anglican, and other traditions. We usually follow the dates that are found in the Episcopal publication called *Lesser Feasts and Fasts, 2006*. This book is also a reference for remembering saints for most days in the year and for children (and adults) to continue to learn more about the saints, using this liturgical orientation.

You can order this book at *www.morehouseeducation.org*
or by calling: 1-800-242-1918.

WHERE TO FIND MATERIALS

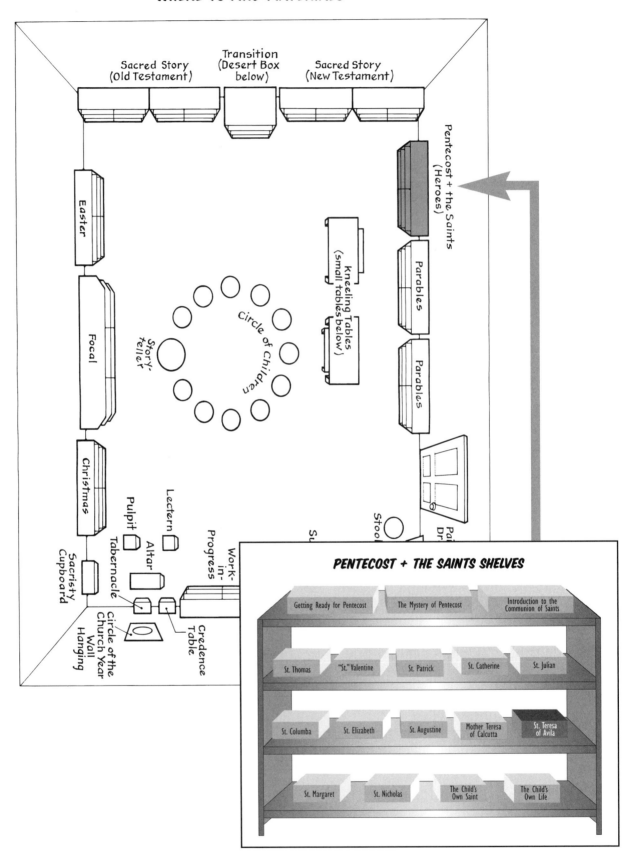

Sacred Story (Old Testament)

Transition (Desert Box below)

Sacred Story (New Testament)

Pentecost + the Saints (Heroes)

Easter

Focal

Story-teller

Circle of Children

Kneeling Tables (small tables below)

Parables

Parables

Christmas

Pulpit

Lectern

Altar

Tabernacle

Work-in-Progress

Stool

Sacristy Cupboard

Circle of the Church Year Wall Hanging

Credence Table

PENTECOST + THE SAINTS SHELVES

| Getting Ready for Pentecost | The Mystery of Pentecost | Introduction to the Communion of Saints |

| St. Thomas | "St." Valentine | St. Patrick | St. Catherine | St. Julian |

| St. Columba | St. Elizabeth | St. Augustine | Mother Teresa of Calcutta | St. Teresa of Avila |

| St. Margaret | St. Nicholas | The Child's Own Saint | The Child's Own Life |

MOVEMENTS	WORDS
Go and get the material for St. Teresa of Avila's story.	Watch where I go to get the lesson for today.
Unfold the underlay in front of you and say:	This is the story of St. Teresa of Avila. The church remembers her during the green and growing time of the church year—after Pentecost. I wonder *why* we remember Teresa? Let's see.
Take the saint booklet from the tray and place it in the center of the underlay.	Teresa was born in the middle part of Spain in the town of Avila. She was one of ten children.
	Her home was a warm and lively place, but when she was only about 12 years old her mother died, and everything changed. When she 14, her father sent her away to school where she discovered she wanted to spend her whole life coming closer and closer to God. How was she going to do that?
Place the bed on the underlay.	She decided to become a Carmelite nun at the age of 22. She entered into her new life with all her heart, but the next year she became very, very sick. Over the next three years she got slowly better, but she still could not walk. Finally, she was well enough to get out of bed, but all her life she had trouble with her health.
	When Teresa was about 40 years old something remarkable happened. She was praying in her regular way when suddenly everything was changed. She felt like God was not only there but more than ever before. She could not see or hear God exactly, but *she knew* God was there, and God was there all the time. This new awareness of God's presence filled her with strength and a wonderful happiness.
	People could tell she had changed. She seemed to be especially happy and sure of herself. Her poor health no longer seemed to make any difference. She was full of playful jokes and loved to visit with everyone.
Place the donkey on the underlay.	In those days people traveled mainly by donkey. If they had more money they could go by mule. If they were especially rich they traveled by horseback or in coaches. Teresa rode on a donkey.
	One day, as she was crossing a river, the saddle she was sitting on began to slip. She was praying while she rode, so she didn't notice what was happening. Suddenly, the saddle went all the way under the donkey and Teresa landed in the water.

MOVEMENTS

Place the crystal on the underlay.

WORDS

She said, "God, why do you treat your friends like this? No wonder you have so few friends," Teresa laughed. The people who were traveling with her wondered whom she was talking to.

Teresa wrote several big books to help people learn what she had discovered about God. One was called *The Interior Castle*. She wrote that coming closer to God is like entering a huge castle made out of very clear crystal in which there are many rooms. Each room has an inner door, which opens to the next room, until you come to the center of the castle. It is so light there that all you can see is God

If you go to Spain today and visit the city of Seville you can still see this book, set like a ruby in a glass case. This book is one of the reasons that Teresa is called a Doctor of the church today, like Catherine of Siena and Theresa of Lisieux.

Teresa's last journey was not especially important, but it was too much for her. When she came to the city of Alba, empty of all her strength, she went to the Carmelite Sisters who gave her a small room. She died there, thanking God that she had been a true daughter of the Church.

We remember Teresa because she was strict, but laughed for God.

COMPLETE LAYOUT OF THE STORY OF ST. TERESA OF AVILA

MOVEMENTS

Guide the wondering about Teresa's life using these wondering questions.

Show the children the booklet. Point out the map of the world showing where Teresa lived, the flag of the country, the time line showing when she lived, and the story printed to help the children know Teresa better.

Model how to put the lesson back on the and then carry it back to its spot on the shelf.

Return to your spot in the circle and begin to dismiss the children to their work.

WORDS

I wonder what parts of Teresa's story you like the best?

I wonder what part of the story is the most important?

I wonder what part of the story is about you or where you might be in the story?

I wonder if we could leave any part of the story out and still have all the story that we need?

Let me show you what is inside this booklet and how you might work with it yourself.

Now let me show you how to put the story away. Here is the bed that reminds us that Teresa was very sick when she first became a nun. Here is the donkey that reminds us of the funny story about Teresa and God laughing together in the river. And here is the crystal that makes us think of Teresa's "picture" of a castle that is so filled with light. Here is the booklet that helps us remember all about Teresa. And here is the green underlay, because we remember Teresa during the green and growing season of the year.

Now I wonder what you would like to make your work today?

THE STORY OF ST. MARGARET OF SCOTLAND (REMEMBERED NOV. 16, DIED IN 1093)

LESSON NOTES

FOCUS: ST. MARGARET OF SCOTLAND CARED FOR HER CHILDREN AND THE PEOPLE OF HER COUNTRY FOR GOD.

THE MATERIAL

- LOCATION: THE MYSTERY OF PENTECOST SHELF, BOTTOM SHELF, UNDER ST. COLUMBA
- PIECES: ST. MARGARET OF SCOTLAND BOOKLET, A PIECE OF TAPESTRY, MODEL OF DUNFERMLINE ABBEY, COINS
- UNDERLAY: GREEN

BACKGROUND

Margaret of Scotland was of Anglo-Saxon, royal blood, so she fled to Scotland to the court of Malcolm when William the Conqueror, a Norman, took England. She married the king and bore him six sons and two daughters. She helped reform the Scottish Catholic Church from Celtic to Roman traditions, reestablished Columba's island of Iona as a holy place, and cared for the poor of Scotland as well as her family.

NOTES ON THE MATERIAL

St. Margaret of Scotland's story sits on a small, shallow tray about 8 inches square, with sides about two inches deep. It has a groove in the front to slide the "saint booklet" in so the children can see it when they approach the Mystery of Pentecost shelf.

The booklet is 4.25" x 5.5". The cover has an image of St. Margaret on it that matches the saint figure used in the introductory lessons on the communion of saints. The second page has a map of the world on it, with Scotland, Margaret's home, highlighted and labeled. It also has an image of the flag of the United Kingdom because Scotland is part of the United Kingdom. The third page has a time line beginning with the year 1 AD and ending with the year 2000 AD. It has an arrow indicating when Margaret lived. The rest of the booklet has the story of the life of Margaret.

Behind the booklet in the tray are placed the objects used to help us remember Margaret's life: a piece of tapestry, a model of Dunfermline Abbey and some coins. The underlay is a 12" square piece of green cloth and is folded on top of the objects.

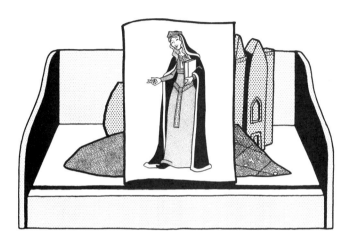

ST. MARGARET OF SCOTLAND TRAY

A NOTE ABOUT DATES FOR THE SAINTS

There is scholarly debate about the dates for the lives of many saints. We have had to make decisions about these dates for pedagogical reasons. We hope the children will continue to learn more about the saints all their life long, including their dates. The basis for the dates used in this volume is how they are remembered liturgically. This has been established by custom in the Roman Catholic, Anglican, and other traditions. We usually follow the dates that are found in the Episcopal publication called *Lesser Feasts and Fasts, 2006*. This book is also a reference for remembering saints for most days in the year and for children (and adults) to continue to learn more about the saints, using this liturgical orientation.

You can order this book at *www.morehouseeducation.org* or by calling: 1-800-242-1918.

WHERE TO FIND MATERIALS

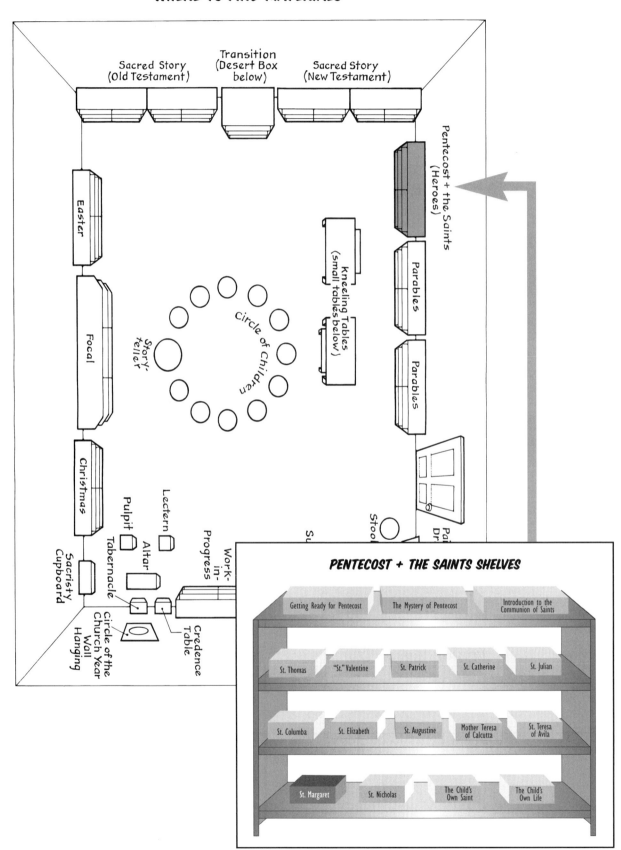

PENTECOST + THE SAINTS SHELVES

Sacred Story (Old Testament)

Transition (Desert Box below)

Sacred Story (New Testament)

Pentecost + the Saints (Heroes)

Easter

Focal

Christmas

Story-teller

circle of Children

kneeling Tables (small tables below)

Parables

Parables

Lectern

Pulpit

Altar

Tabernacle

Work-in-Progress

Credence Table

Circle of the Church Year Wall Hanging

Sacristy Cupboard

Stool

Getting Ready for Pentecost | The Mystery of Pentecost | Introduction to the Communion of Saints

St. Thomas | "St." Valentine | St. Patrick | St. Catherine | St. Julian

St. Columba | St. Elizabeth | St. Augustine | Mother Teresa of Calcutta | St. Teresa of Avila

St. Margaret | St. Nicholas | The Child's Own Saint | The Child's Own Life

MOVEMENTS	WORDS
Go and get the material for St. Margaret of Scotland's story.	Watch where I go to get the lesson for today.
Unfold the underlay in front of you and say:	This is the story of St. Margaret of Scotland. The church remembers her during the green and growing time of the church year—after Pentecost. I wonder *why* we remember Margaret? Let's see.
Take the saint booklet from the tray and place it in the center of the underlay.	Margaret of Scotland was born in Hungary, but she moved to England when she was 12.
	She lived happily in England until William the Conqueror took the country. William did not want anyone from the family of the old kings in the palace, so Margaret fled to Scotland when she was 22.
	The King of Scotland was named Malcolm. He understood about leaving home because he had to flee for his life when his own father King Duncan had been murdered by Macbeth. He welcomed the beautiful princess and fell in love with her. They were married three years later.
Place the piece of tapestry on the underlay.	They had eight children together and Margaret was a wonderful mother. She turned the cold and grim palace into a warm and happy home. She hung bright tapestries over the stones of the palace walls and added many beautiful books to the library.
	Margaret never managed to teach Malcolm how to read, but she did persuade him that books were important. Even though the King could not read the Bible, people saw him kiss it to show his respect.
	Margaret cared deeply about her religion. In the palace there was a place for her to pray. Soon other people in the palace began to join her in her prayers, and she made sure that the servants had time to come and pray too.
Place the model of Dunfermline Abbey on the underlay.	She also helped the clergy in the church do their job more beautifully. She rebuilt the monastery on the Island of Iona and brought the Benedictine monks to Scotland. She built them a home at Dunfermline Abbey.

MOVEMENTS

Place the coins on the underlay.

WORDS

Every day she opened the doors of the palace to everyone, especially the poor. When she traveled around Scotland she also gave money to the poor. She gave away so much money that Malcolm grew concerned. But over time, he knew this was the right thing to do. The King trusted her so much, he asked her questions about how to rule Scotland.

Then a great war broke out between Scotland and England. Malcolm led the Scottish army against the English, but was defeated. He was killed, and so was their oldest son. Margaret was ill at this time. When a younger son came back from the battle she asked how everyone was. He said they were fine, but she knew the truth. Four days later she prayed to God, "Let me be free." That was the day of her death. She was buried at Dunfermline Abbey.

We remember Margaret because she cared for her own children and the people of her country for God.

COMPLETE LAYOUT OF THE STORY OF ST. MARGARET OF SCOTLAND

MOVEMENTS

Guide the wondering about Margaret's life using these wondering questions.

Show the children the booklet. Point out the map of the world showing where Margaret lived, the flag of the country, the time line showing when she lived, and the story printed to help the children know Margaret better.

Model how to put the lesson back on the tray and then carry it back to its spot on the shelf.

Return to your spot on the circle and begin to dismiss the children to their work.

WORDS

I wonder what parts of Margaret's story you like the best?

I wonder what part of the story is the most important?

I wonder what part of the story is about you or where you might be in the story?

I wonder if we could leave any part of the story out and still have all the story that we need?

Let me show you what is inside this booklet and how you might work with it yourself.

Now let me show you how to put the story away. Here is the tapestry that reminds us that Margaret made the palace a beautiful place to live. Here is Dunfermline Abbey that reminds us how much Margaret loved to pray and how she gave the Benedictine monks a home there. Here are some coins that remind us that Margaret loved to help the poor of Scotland. Here is the booklet that helps us remember all about Margaret. And here is the green underlay, because we remember Margaret during the green and growing season of the year.

Now I wonder what you would like to make your work today?

THE STORY OF ST. NICHOLAS, BISHOP OF MYRA

(REMEMBERED DEC. 6, DIED ABOUT 343)

LESSON NOTES

FOCUS: ST. NICHOLAS GAVE GIFTS FOR GOD.

THE MATERIAL

- LOCATION: THE MYSTERY OF PENTECOST SHELF, BOTTOM SHELF, BESIDE ST. MARGARET
- PIECES: ST. NICHOLAS, BISHOP OF MYRA BOOKLET, CHRIST CHILD IN THE MANGER, BISHOP'S MITER, WRAPPED PRESENT
- UNDERLAY—PURPLE OR BLUE

BACKGROUND

St. Nicholas was the bishop of Myra, which is now in southern Turkey. He died about 343 and was buried in Myra. In 1087 Italian sailors moved his body to Bari, which is today on the East Coast of Italy. This is why he is sometimes known as St. Nicholas of Bari. There are many stories about this popular saint, but he is best known for giving gifts in secret to children.

NOTES ON THE MATERIAL

St. Nicholas's story sits on a small, shallow tray about 8 inches square, with sides about two inches deep. It has a groove in the front to slide the "saint booklet" in so the children can see it when they approach the Mystery of Pentecost shelf.

The booklet is 4.25" x 5.5". The cover has an image of St. Nicholas on it that matches the saint figure used in the introductory lessons on the communion of saints. The second page has a map of the world on it, with Turkey, Nicholas's home, highlighted and labeled. It also has an image of the flag of Turkey. The third page has a time line beginning with the year 1 AD and ending with the year 2000 AD. It has an arrow indicating when Nicholas lived. The rest of the booklet has the story of the life of Nicholas.

Behind the booklet in the tray are placed the objects used to help us remember Nicholas's life: the Christ child in the manger, a bishop's miter and a wrapped present. The underlay is a 12" square piece of purple or blue cloth (use the color your community uses to "mark" the season of Advent) and is folded on top of the objects.

ST. NICHOLAS, BISHOP OF MYRA TRAY

A NOTE ABOUT DATES FOR THE SAINTS

There is scholarly debate about the dates for the lives of many saints. We have had to make decisions about these dates for pedagogical reasons. We hope the children will continue to learn more about the saints all their life long, including their dates. The basis for the dates used in this volume is how they are remembered liturgically. This has been established by custom in the Roman Catholic, Anglican, and other traditions. We usually follow the dates that are found in the Episcopal publication called *Lesser Feasts and Fasts, 2006*. This book is also a reference for remembering saints for most days in the year and for children (and adults) to continue to learn more about the saints, using this liturgical orientation.

You can order this book at *www.morehouseeducation.org* or by calling: 1-800-242-1918.

WHERE TO FIND MATERIALS

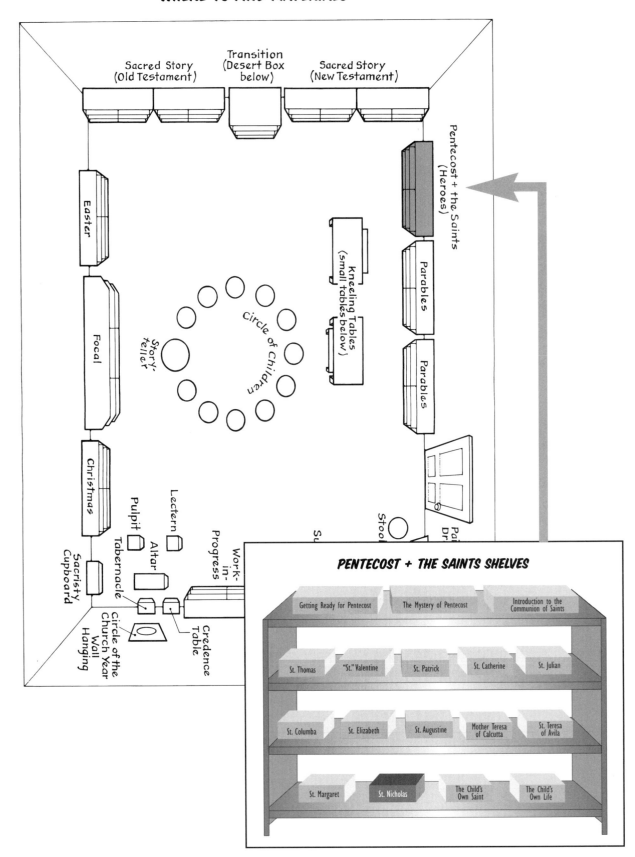

Sacred Story (Old Testament)

Transition (Desert Box below)

Sacred Story (New Testament)

Pentecost + the Saints (Heroes)

Easter

Focal

Christmas

Kneeling Tables (small tables below)

Parables

Parables

Story-teller

Circle of Children

Sacristy Cupboard

Pulpit

Lectern

Altar

Tabernacle

Work-in-Progress

Circle of the Church Year Wall Hanging

Credence Table

PENTECOST + THE SAINTS SHELVES

Getting Ready for Pentecost

The Mystery of Pentecost

Introduction to the Communion of Saints

St. Thomas

"St." Valentine

St. Patrick

St. Catherine

St. Julian

St. Columba

St. Elizabeth

St. Augustine

Mother Teresa of Calcutta

St. Teresa of Avila

St. Margaret

St. Nicholas

The Child's Own Saint

The Child's Own Life

MOVEMENTS	WORDS
Go and get the material for St. Nicholas's story.	Watch where I go to get the lesson for today.
Unfold the underlay in front of you and say:	This is the story of St. Nicholas. The church remembers him during Advent, the time for getting ready to come close to the mystery of Christmas. I wonder *why* we remember Nicholas?
Take the saint booklet from the tray and place it in the center of the underlay.	There was once a little boy whose mother and father died when he was only a child. He always wanted to give a present to the Christ Child, but the Christ Child lived long before little Nicholas was born. Still he wondered if the Christ Child was living in every child.
Place the Christ Child on the underlay.	
Place the bishop's miter on the underlay.	Nicholas became a priest. People knew he was a holy person, so they made him their Bishop. The place where he was a bishop was in Myra, a city in the south of a country we now call Turkey.
Place the wrapped gift on the underlay.	Nicholas was shy. When he began to give gifts to children on Christmas Eve he did it in secret so no one would know.

Sometimes the gifts came down the chimney. Sometimes they were left by the door. Sometimes they were dropped in through an open window. Nicholas would tiptoe away in the night leaving the delight of the gift to be enjoyed in the morning.

When Nicholas grew older it was hard for him to give gifts on Christmas Eve and even to give the people the holy bread and wine in the church. The people carried him to church so that he could keep sharing the holy bread and wine with him.

When Nicholas died something amazing happened. The gifts which people had found in their homes on Christmas day continued to appear.

One day the Emperor of Russia heard this story. He decided to make Nicholas the patron saint of Russia. Far in the north of Russia where there was nothing but snow, gifts continued to appear. The story traveled westward into Finland, and Sweden, and Norway where the reindeer lived.

MOVEMENTS	WORDS

WORDS

The story continued to spread and came to Holland. When Dutch people came to this country they brought the story with them. Presents began to appear here too, and they still do to this day.

This all began with the gifts of the poor bishop of Myra for the children of his town, because he saw the Christ child in every child.

We remember Nicholas because he gave gifts for God.

COMPLETE LAYOUT OF THE STORY OF ST. NICHOLAS, BISHOP OF MYRA

Guide the wondering about Nicholas's life using these wondering questions.

I wonder what parts of Nicholas's story you like the best?

I wonder what part of the story is the most important?

I wonder what part of the story is about you or where you might be in the story?

I wonder if we could leave any part of the story out and still have all the story that we need?

MOVEMENTS	WORDS
Show the children the booklet. Point out the map of the world showing where Nicholas lived, the flag of the country, the time line showing when he lived, and the story printed to help the children know Nicholas better.	Let me show you what is inside this booklet and how you might work with it yourself.
Model how to put the lesson back on the tray and then carry it back to its spot on the shelf.	Now let me show you how to put the story away. Here is the Christ Child that reminds us that Nicholas always wanted to give gifts to the Christ Child in every child. Here is the bishop's miter, the special hat that bishops like Nicholas wear. And here is the gift that reminds us of all the gifts Nicholas gave, and the gifts that are still given even though Nicholas is now gone. And here is the purple (or blue) underlay, because we remember Nicholas during the season of Advent, the time for getting ready to come close to the mystery of Christmas.
Return to your place in the circle and begin to dismiss the children to their work.	Now I wonder what you would like to make your work today?

LESSON 15

THE STORY OF THE CHILD'S OWN SAINT

LESSON NOTES

FOCUS: WE ALL KNOW PEOPLE WHO ARE SAINTS.

THE MATERIAL

- **LOCATION: THE MYSTERY OF PENTECOST SHELF, BOTTOM SHELF, NEXT TO ST. NICHOLAS**
- **PIECES: THE CHILD WILL DECIDE.**
- **UNDERLAY: THE CHILD WILL DECIDE.**

BACKGROUND

There are many saints that have been recognized by the church and there are many that are known only to God. There is the possibility within each of us to be a saint, so it is only natural that children may have known people in their lives who are holy, and would like to celebrate as a saint.

NOTES ON THE MATERIAL

The child will create this lesson. The only thing you will provide is a tray for it, like the other saint trays. You should keep one empty tray on the shelf beside St. Nicholas's story to leave the possibility of this lesson open. You'll need extras in a closet nearby for all of the children. You will need cloth in the different colors for each season of the church year available, and scissors for cutting the underlay the right size. In addition, we suggest you have cloth, felt, clay, paint, wood, glue and other art supplies available, from which the child can create objects for this lesson. You will also want a book the children can use to look up the flag of the country where their saint lives or lived.

SPECIAL NOTES

You can present this lesson to the whole circle of children, a small group, or to an individual child. You must be sure you have enough supplies for everyone if you decide to tell it to the whole group at once.

WHERE TO FIND MATERIALS

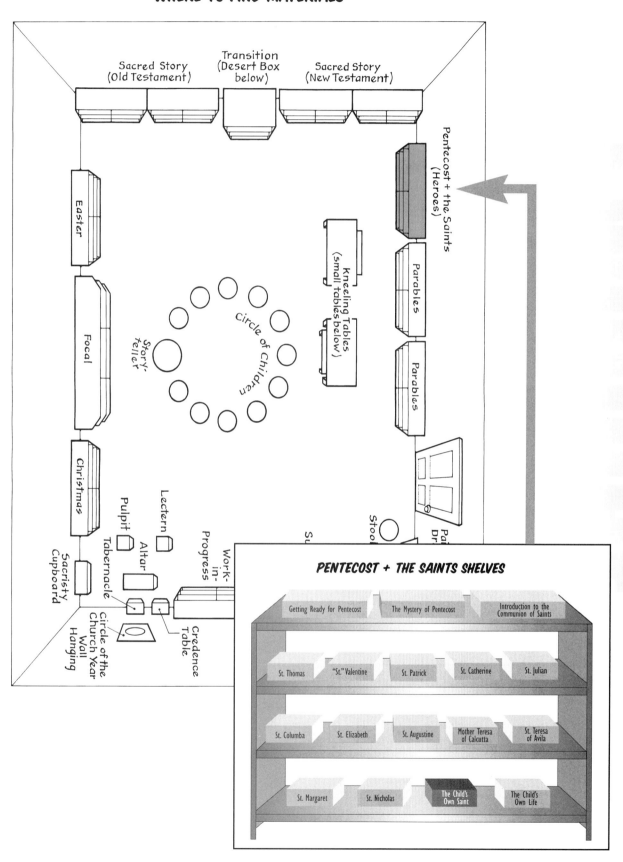

Sacred Story (Old Testament)

Transition (Desert Box below)

Sacred Story (New Testament)

Pentecost + the Saints (Heroes)

Easter

Focal

Christmas

Story-teller

Circle of Children

kneeling Tables (small tables below)

Parables

Parables

Lectern

Pulpit

Altar

Tabernacle

Sacristy Cupboard

Circle of the Church Year Wall Hanging

Credence Table

Work-in-Progress

Stool

PENTECOST + THE SAINTS SHELVES

Getting Ready for Pentecost

The Mystery of Pentecost

Introduction to the Communion of Saints

St. Thomas

"St." Valentine

St. Patrick

St. Catherine

St. Julian

St. Columba

St. Elizabeth

St. Augustine

Mother Teresa of Calcutta

St. Teresa of Avila

St. Margaret

St. Nicholas

The Child's Own Saint

The Child's Own Life

MOVEMENTS	WORDS
Sit quietly with the child or group of children for a moment until they are ready to listen. You then speak slowly, carefully, and with great respect.	There are saints that the church knows, and there are some saints known only to God. It could be that you know one of these unnamed saints. I wonder if you would like to make a story about that person? It could be someone who is old or young, a mom or a dad—anyone. It could be someone who is fun, or someone who is serious, or someone who is both. It could be someone who is important, or it could be someone most people don't even notice. There are all kinds of saints, but everyone is someone who is known by God. Sometimes saints are alive and sometimes saints are dead. The ones we've been remembering are dead, but the person you remember may still be alive.
Point to the "Circle of the Church Year" hanging on the wall.	We need to put this person in the church year, so we'll use his or her birthday. This will help us mark the person's time now. Then we'll know what color to make the underlay.
Help the child find the right time in the church year and its corresponding color.	Why don't you go and get a rug and put it in just the right place, then go and get the empty box that is sitting on the shelf and put it on the rug. You can then make a lesson about your own saint.
Show the children where the supplies are kept for making the underlays.	You need to cut out an underlay. You need to make a booklet and objects to go in the box. All of the supplies you need are on our art supply shelves.
Get two pieces of paper (8.5"x11"), one for you to use and one for the child. Model how to fold the paper.	Let me show you how to make the booklet. Get a piece of paper and then fold it once like this, and then like this. Now it has one, two, three, four pages. On the first page you put a picture of the person you want to remember. On the second page you make a map. Put a red dot where the person lives and make the flag of the country where you would go to meet that person.
Show the child where the book is kept in your classroom.	Here is a book you can use to find out what the flag should look like. On the third page you make a time line and put down as much as you know.

MOVEMENTS

WORDS

On the last page you write a paragraph or tell the story to someone who can write things down for you.

Finally, see if you can make three objects to put in this tray that help us remember what is special about this person.

You could make something from what we have on our art shelves, or you might find something at home to bring to put in the tray.

You don't have to finish it today. When it is finished you can tell it to a friend or to me. You can tell it to our whole class. You can take it home. You can keep it in your room. You could even give it to the person it is about. You can use it anyway you want. It is about your own special person.

If you have been working with a child individually you can end here. If you have made this a group presentation you will need to pause now and look around the circle. Speak slowly and with feeling.

****

There are many things in this room that you can make your work today. You may even have unfinished work you would like to finish. Making your own lesson about someone special to you is very good work too, if you would like to choose it.

Dismiss the children one by one to go get out their work after it has been carefully chosen.

Now, what work would you like to get out today?

LESSON 16
THE STORY OF THE CHILD'S OWN LIFE

LESSON NOTES

FOCUS: EACH PERSON HAS THE POSSIBILITY THROUGH THE GRACE OF GOD TO LIVE A HOLY LIFE.

THE MATERIAL

- **LOCATION: THE MYSTERY OF PENTECOST SHELF, BOTTOM SHELF, NEXT TO THE CHILD'S OWN SAINT**
- **PIECES: THE CHILD WILL DETERMINE THIS.**
- **UNDERLAY: THE CHILD WILL DETERMINE THIS.**

BACKGROUND

There are saints who are known only to God. None of us really know who will be saint but each person has the possibility through the grace of God to live a holy life. So, all of the children are included in the communion of saints, and they need to know this.

NOTES ON THE MATERIAL

The child will create this lesson. The only thing you will provide is a tray for it, like the other saint trays. You should keep a second empty tray on the shelf beside the one for the child's own saint. Leave the possibility of this lesson open. You'll need extras in a closet nearby for all of the children. You will need cloth in the different colors for each season of the church year available, and scissors for cutting the underlays the right size. In addition, we suggest you have cloth, felt, clay, paint, wood, glue and other art supplies available from which the child can create objects for this lesson.

SPECIAL NOTES

You can present this lesson to the whole circle of children, a small group or to an individual child. You must be sure you have enough supplies for everyone if you decide to tell it to the whole group at once.

WHERE TO FIND MATERIALS

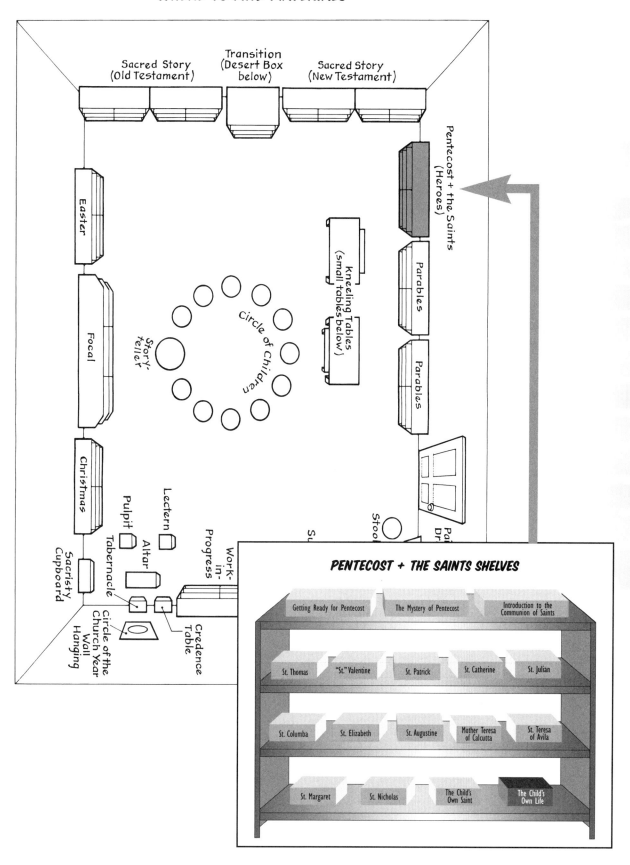

Sacred Story (Old Testament)

Transition (Desert Box below)

Sacred Story (New Testament)

Pentecost + the Saints (Heroes)

Easter

Focal

Christmas

Sacristy Cupboard

Circle of the Church Year Wall Hanging

Tabernacle

Altar

Pulpit

Lectern

Work-in-Progress

Credence Table

Story-teller

Circle of Children

Kneeling Tables (small tables below)

Parables

Parables

PENTECOST + THE SAINTS SHELVES

Getting Ready for Pentecost

The Mystery of Pentecost

Introduction to the Communion of Saints

St. Thomas | "St." Valentine | St. Patrick | St. Catherine | St. Julian

St. Columba | St. Elizabeth | St. Augustine | Mother Teresa of Calcutta | St. Teresa of Avila

St. Margaret | St. Nicholas | The Child's Own Saint | The Child's Own Life

MOVEMENTS

Sit quietly with the child or group of children for a moment until they are ready to listen. You then speak slowly, carefully, and with great respect.

Help the child figure out what time of the church year he or she was born. Show the child where the supplies are kept to make the underlay.

Get two pieces of paper (8.5" x11"), one for you to use and one for the child. Model how to fold the paper.

Show the child where the book is kept in your classroom.

WORDS

Anyone can be a saint. Perhaps you are one or will be one. People don't always know, they just try to be the best people they can be.

Why don't you make a saint box about yourself just in case?

Go and get a rug. Put it in just the right place. Then go and get the empty box that is sitting on the shelf and put it on the rug.

You need to make a booklet and objects to go in the box. The underlay will be the color of your time, the time when you were born.

Let me show you how to make the booklet.

Get a piece of paper and then fold it once like this, and then like this. Now it has one, two, three, four pages.

On the first page put a picture of you!

On the second page you make a map and put a red dot where you live and make a flag of the country where you live.

Here is a book you can use to find out what the flag should look like.

On the third page you make a time line and put down as much as you know.

On the last page you write a paragraph about yourself or tell the story to someone who can write things down for you.

Finally, see if you can make three objects to put in this tray that help us to remember what is special about you.

You could make something from what we have on our art shelves, or you might find something at home. You don't have to finish it today. When it is finished you can tell it to a friend or to me. You can tell it to the whole class. You can take it home. You can keep it in your room. You can use it anyway you want. It's about your own life.

MOVEMENTS

If you have been working with a child individually you can end here. If you have made this a group presentation you will need to pause now and look around the circle. Speak slowly and with feeling.

Dismiss the children one by one to go get out their work after it has been carefully chosen.

WORDS

****

There are many things in this room that you can make your work today. You may even have unfinished work you would like to finish. Making your own lesson about someone special to you is very good work too, if you would like to choose it.

Now, what work would you like to get out today?